THE COINS
OF THE
SULTANS OF DEHLI
IN THE
BRITISH MUSEUM

THE COINS
OF THE
SULTANS OF DEHLI
IN THE
BRITISH MUSEUM

STANLEY LANE-POOLE, REGINALD S. POOLE

GYAN

Published by

GYAN

Gyan Publishing House
5, Ansari Road
Daryaganj, New Delhi-110002
Phone: 011-47034999, 9811692060
E-mail: books@gyanbooks.com

Distribution Network
gyanbooks.com
India, USA, Canada, UK, Australia

ISBN: 978-93-7133-556-0 (PB)

First Published, 1884

2nd Impression 2025

Printed at: Gyan Press, Delhi.

THE COINS OF THE SULTANS OF DEHLI IN THE BRITISH MUSEUM

Author Stanley Lane-Poole, Reginald S. Poole

CATALOGUE

OF

INDIAN COINS

IN THE

BRITISH MUSEUM.

THE SULTÁNS OF DEHLÍ.

1884.

THE COINS

OF THE

SULTÁNS OF DEHLÍ

IN THE

BRITISH MUSEUM.

BY

STANLEY LANE-POOLE,

B.A., OXON., M.R.A.S.

EDITED BY

REGINALD STUART POOLE, LL.D.

CORRESPONDENT OF THE INSTITUTE OF FRANCE.

1884.

EDITOR'S PREFACE.

The Catalogue of Indian Coins, of which the present volume is the first instalment, will consist primarily of five volumes, of which two, those dealing (1) with the coins of the so-called Patán Sultáns of Dehlí, and (2) with the contemporary issues of the Kings of Bengal, Jaunpúr, Gujarát, and other Arabic coinages, will be the work of the author of the Catalogue of Oriental Coins, Mr. Stanley Lane-Poole, while the earlier series, Greek-Indian and Hindú, will be comprised in two volumes by Prof. Percy Gardner; and I shall myself undertake the description of the currency of the Emperors of Dehlí of the House of Bábar.

The general principles upon which the Catalogue of Indian Coins will be arranged will be similar to those which have been observed in the Greek and Oriental series, but the tabular or column-arrangement which was used in the eighth volume of the Oriental Catalogue will be retained in preference to the open pages of the earlier volumes of that series, save when the length of the inscriptions render the open page necessary.

The coins included in the present volume correspond to Fraehn's Class XVII.

The metal of each specimen is stated, and its size in inches and tenths of inches. The weight of the gold and silver examples is given in English grains. Tables for converting grains into grammes, and inches into millimètres as well as into the measures of Mionnet's scale, are given at the end of the volume.

A comparative table of the years of the Hijrah and of the Christian Era has been added with a view to facilitating reference to the standard works on Indian history where the European computation is adopted.

Typical specimens are figured in the nine plates, which are executed by the autotype mechanical process from casts in plaster.

The work has been written by Mr. Stanley Lane-Poole, and I have carefully revised it throughout, except in the case of the Nágarí inscriptions, which have been collated by Mr. Gardner.

REGINALD STUART POOLE.

INTRODUCTION.

The present volume comprises the coinage of the Sultáns commonly known as the "Patán" or "Pathán" Kings of Dehlí. With some reluctance I have abandoned this time-honoured designation, for the reason that the word Patán is synonymous with Afghán, and most of the Sultáns of Dehlí were not Afgháns. The founder of the line of Dehlí, Muhammad ibn Sám, was a *Ghórí Turk;* and his successors, the rest of the first dynasty, were his Turkish slaves and their offspring. The second dynasty, sprung from Jalál-ad-dín Fíróz Sháh, was composed of *Khaljí Turks.* The third dynasty, that of the Taghlak-Sháhís, was of the race of the *Játs.* The fourth claimed descent from the Arab Husain, grandson of the prophet Muhammad, and called itself by the sacred title of *Sayyids.* Indeed, only the fifth and the sixth of the dynasties into which the kings of Dehlí are divided could properly term themselves Patán or Afghán, inasmuch as Buhlól belonged to the Lódí tribe of Afgháns, and Shér Sháh to the Súr division of the Lódí tribe. Thus, out of forty Sultáns of Dehlí, eight alone have any right to be called Patáns or Afgháns. If, therefore, the name is to be retained at all in this misleading connection, it can only be in deference to long-established usage. The gain in convenience, however, in thus preserving the appellation, is surely more than counterbalanced by the historical and ethnological accuracy which is restored by its abolition.

The series of coins struck by the Sultáns of Dehlí offer fewer points of interest and importance than do most of the currencies of Muhammadan States. As a rule we may look upon Muhammadan coins as the surest foundations for an exact history of the dynasties by which they were issued. The coins of a Muslim ruler generally go far to establish those outward data in regard to his reign which Oriental historians too often neglect or misstate. The year of accession, the extent of his dominion, his relations with the neighbouring powers and with the spiritual chief of his religion, are all facts for which we may look with confidence to his coins. In many of the smaller and less known dynasties it is hardly too much to say that the coins are our chief informers. Unfortunately we cannot claim this importance for the issues of the Sultáns of Dehlí. The history of this dynasty has been recorded in detail by native writers, to whose statements the coins can add but little that is new or valuable. Now and again the coinage may suffice to establish the truth about a disputed date, but such examples of usefulness are rare in the series. Moreover, owing to the habit with weak rulers, whose tenure of power was unusually precarious, of protecting themselves behind the ægis of a renowned predecessor, and issuing their coins in the name of a deceased but revered Sultán, it is not always easy to feel assured that the dates on the coins represent precisely what they profess; and to arrange the order and years of the succession by these dates, without reference to the histories, would create no little confusion. Almost the only piece of historical information which has been thought to be derived from the coins alone is the presumed issue of the piece No. 85 in this volume, by Násir-ad-dín Mahmúd, the eldest son of Altamsh, during his father's lifetime. This would doubtless be interesting if it were established, but the result of a careful examination of the facts has led me to reject, with all diffidence, Mr. Thomas's attribution. Two sons of Sultán Altamsh bore the title of Násir-ad-dín; the elder was governor of Bengal from 624 to 626, when he died: the younger, born in the year of his brother's death, became Sultán of Dehlí after Mas'úd Sháh, and reigned from 644 to 664. Mr. Thomas ascribes the coin No. 85 to the short government of Bengal by the elder Násir-ad-dín, on the ground of the occurrence upon it of the name of the 'Abbásí Khalífah Al-Mustansir, who reigned from 623 to 640. The improbability of the governor's striking coins in his own name, without any acknowledgment of his father, the reigning Sultán Altamsh, together with the close resemblance between this coin and those which undoubtedly belong to the younger Násir-ad-dín, led me to class No. 85 among the latter's coinage, and to regard the anachronism of the Khalífah's name as merely an instance of the not unfrequent posthumous use of names on Dehlí coins. Since coming to this decision, I notice that Dr. A. F. R. Hoernle* has arrived at the same conclusion, and has supported his view by some cogent arguments, the substance of which I here reproduce. In the first place, no Governor of Bengal, unless he had thrown off the yoke of Dehlí, ever substituted his own name for that of his master the Sultán. The utmost a governor might do was to add his name after his master's, as Yildiz did after Muhammad ibn Sám's. Secondly, coins probably struck in Bengal, and clearly dated 624, do not bear Násir-ad-dín's name. It is evident that when the latter styles himself *Sultán*, and puts his own name exclusively on the coin, he does not do so as a mere governor. Moreover, the publication by Dr. Hoernle in the same article of a coin of 'Alá-ad-dín Mas'úd, with precisely the same obverse, including the peculiar للّه and the omission of the article before *Sultán*, seems to put it beyond a doubt that Násir-ad-dín copied his obverse from his immediate predecessor, at first, and that the coin No. 85 was his earliest issue. Neither the coin of Mas'úd nor No. 85 have any trace of marginal inscriptions or dates.

* *Journal of the Asiatic Society of Bengal*, vol. l., 1881, pp. 62—65.

A certain historical value attaches to the joint issues of Fíróz III. and his sons Fath and Zafar, as confirming the notices of the historians. Fíróz "invested his son Fath with the insignia of royalty in 760, and placed his name, in conjunction with his own, on the public currency," as Ferishtah records; and the Egyptian Khalífah Al-Mu'tadid sent a robe of investiture to the young prince. All this is confirmed by the inscriptions on the coins, where we find the names of the Sultán and his son and the Khalífah conjointly on all specimens. On the other hand, while the coins also corroborate the statements of the historians as to the succession of Zafar, another son of Fíróz III., to Fath's place, on the death of that prince, the value of the numismatic data is considerably diminished by the occurrence of one of those too common instances of posthumous issues which destroy to some extent the trustworthiness of the Dehlí currency as historical evidence. No. 387 bears the date 791, when Zafar was no longer alive: and the hypothesis of Mr. Rodgers that it may refer to a son of Zafar, who bore the same name, seems far-fetched.

The coinage of the Sultáns of Dehlí is more valuable from the point of view of political geography. Mr. Thomas, in his classical account of the *Chronicles of the Pathán Kings of Dehlí*, thus describes the first foundation of the dynasty, and the beginning of the acquisition of that wide dominion which reached its greatest extent under the famous Muhammad ibn Taghlak.

"The later scions of the dynasty of Sabaktagín, driven out of Ghazní on its sack by 'Alá-ad-dín Husain Jahánsóz in A.H. 550, retired to Láhór, and had already, in effect, become domesticated Indian sovereigns; so that, as Mu'izz-ad-dín pressed down and around them, the occupation of the more advanced provinces of Hindústán followed as a natural sequence. Mu'izz-ad-dín Muhammad ibn Sám, or Shibáb-ad-dín as he was called in his youth, otherwise known as Muhammad Ghórí, the founder of the Patháu dynasty of Dehlí, is first noticed in history on the occasion of his nomination, in conjunction with his elder brother, Ghiyás-ad-dín, to the charge of a province of Ghór, by his uncle, the notorious 'Alá-ad-dín Husain Jahánsóz. After the accession of Ghiyás-ad-dín to the throne of Ghór, in 558 A.H., Mu'izz-ad-dín, acting as his general, subdued portions of Khurásán; and, on the conquest of Ghazní in 569, he was nominated by his suzerain brother to the government of that country. From this time his incursions into India commenced: in 571 he conquered Multán; in 574 he experienced a sanguinary defeat in an expedition against the prince of Nahrwála; next, Khusrú Malik, the last of the Ghaznavís, was assailed, and at length in 583 captured by stratagem. In 587, in a more extended expedition into Hindústán, Muhammad Ghórí was totally routed on the memorable field of Thaneswar by the Chohán leader, Prithví Rája of Ajmír. After a year's repose, the disgrace of this defeat still rankling within him, he, on the self-same battle-ground, again encountered his former adversary, now supported by the whole force of the country, the confederated armies of 150 princes. This time fortune favoured the Ghórís, and a hard-fought field terminated in the total discomfiture of the Indian host. By this single victory the Muhammadans may be said to have become the virtual masters of Hindústán. The ulterior measures for the subjugation of the country were of speedy accomplishment, and most of the later additions to the Indian empire of Muhammad Ghórí were perfected by his quondam slave, subsequent representative in Hindústán, and eventual successor on the throne of Dehlí, Kutb-ad-dín Aibek. Ghiyás-ad-dín, who had long retained little beyond the title of a king, died in 599 A.H., and shortly afterwards Mu'izz-ad-dín was installed in form. An unsuccessful attempt at conquest in the north, in itself attended by most disastrous results, was succeeded by the revolt of the governors of Ghazní and Multán: this outbreak, however, was soon suppressed. In the month of Sha'bán, A.H. 602, Muhammad Ghórí was slain in his tent, in the centre of his own camp, by a band of Gakkars. At his death, the Muslim empire of India extended generally over nearly the whole of Hindústán proper, Sind, and Bengal. The sovereignty was, however, held by very exceptional tenures, and was most indeterminate in its inner geographical limits."*

This wide empire, although it underwent many temporary retrogressions, gradually advanced in extent up to the time of Muhammad ibn Taghlak, when, according to the account of Siráj-ad-dín 'Umar of Oudh,† it included the following provinces:

Dehlí.	Oudh.
Deógír.	Kanauj.
Multán.	Lakhnautí.
Kohrám.	Bihár.
Samánah.	Karrah.
Siwistán (Sehwán).	Málwah.
Úchh.	Láhór.
Hánsí.	Kalánúr.
Sirsutí.	Jájnagar.
Malabár.	Telingana.
Gujarát.	Dwára Samundra.
Badáón.	

A reference to the map of India, facing page xvi, will show the vast extent of the dominion included in these provinces. But the elements of dissolution are always present in a huge and disconnected congeries of states. Muhammad ibn Taghlak, in spite of his extraordinary perversity, was no ordinary ruler, and he, if any one, had the will and the power to hold his unwieldy empire together. But the circumstances were too strong even for his iron resolution.

* E. Thomas: *Chronicles*, pp. 10—12.

† Notices et Extraits, xiii. 170, *cf.* Thomas, p. 203.

"The dominion covering twenty-three provinces, or independent nationalities, became, in the very number of its sections, essentially incoherent. Local feudatories had of late been superseded by governors appointed by the head of the state, and the selection of fitting and trustworthy representatives was attended by far greater risks than of old, now that the national bond, so effective among the ruling classes under the dynasty of the Turks, had disappeared amid the dissensions of Turk and Khiljí, both of whom had henceforth to bow to an alien Sultán of curiously mixed breed. In the Muhammadan distrust of unconverted Hindús, all manner of foreign adventurers were installed in divisional posts: these men, having little or no interest in the stability of the throne, were ever ready to aid any projected rising or to join with their combined forces any of the more influential rebels. So that the annals of the period present a mere succession of outbreaks,—no sooner was one section of the empire brought back to its allegiance than another division would seek to assert its independence.

"The Sultán was often obliged to command his own armies; and though he was usually victorious, the very fact of his absence in distant parts encouraged the disaffected elsewhere. The old proverb, 'Dehlí is distant,' found a new application; the royal forces were often less near to the threatened point than the inconveniently situated capital itself, whose distance from the southern states had already suggested its supersession by the more central Deógír. A parallel obstacle to the permanent subjection of the provinces was to be found in the state of the roads, and the general insecurity of the country at large, evils that extended to such an extreme that the tribute of the south was allowed to accumulate at Deógír, merely because it was found impossible to transport it to Dehlí, and eventually the whole treasure was divided on the spot among some temporarily successful insurgents.

"The end of such a state of things might easily be predicted. The Bengal mints occupied themselves in coining money for independent rulers; the Sultán's early triumph, Warangol, reverted to its ancient name in the hands of other masters; Deógír, his chosen capital, submitted to Hasan Gángú, the founder of a new race of Kings, the Bahmaní Dynasty of Kulbarga, who were destined to play a prominent part in the destinies of the country; and finally, the owner of so many kingdoms died miserably of a fever, near Thata, on the lower Indus, with his army, "like ants or locusts" around him; and his cousin and successor found some difficulty in getting safe home to the cherished Dehlí, which Muhammad ibn Taghlak had once done so much to desolate and destroy."*

Less than fifty years afterwards, the reigning Sultán of Dehlí, Mahmúd ibn Muhammad, was confined to the capital itself, hemmed in by rival pretenders to the throne from which Muhammad ibn Taghlak had dispensed his erratic notions of law to so immense an empire: and after Tímúr's invasion, 801 A.H., the kingdom of Dehlí was distributed piecemeal, and Ikbál Khán held Dehlí and the Doáb; Zafar Khán, Gujarát; Khizr Khán, Multán, Daibalpúr, and Sind; Khawájah-i-Jahán, Kanauj, Oudh, Karrah, Dalamau, Sandalah, Bahráích, Bihár, and Jaunpúr; Mahmúd Khán, Mahobah and Kálpí; Dilawar Khán, Dhár; Ghálib Khán, Samánah; and Shams Khán, Bíána. Shér Sháh for a moment gathered together once more the fragments of the empire; but it was reserved for Akbar to rebuild the fabric in more than its ancient grandeur.

The coins are of some value in tracing the variations in the empire which thus rose and fell with such astonishing rapidity. With a view to supplying the data they afford in the manner most convenient for reference, I have

* E. Thomas: *Chronicles*, pp. 203—206.

arranged the known mints of each Sultán in the following table, including not only the British Museum examples, but those in Mr. Thomas's *Chronicles*, and in Mr. C. J. Rodgers' supplementary papers in the *Journal* of the Bengal Asiatic Society, vols. xlix. and li.

TABLE ILLUSTRATING THE EXTENT OF THE EMPIRE BY THE MINTS.*

589—602	Muhammad ibn Sám,	Ghazní, [Kanauj,] *Peshawar*, FARWÁN.
	Yildiz,	Ghazní.
607—633	Altamsh,	Dehlí, Multán, Narwar? LÁHÓR?
634—637	Rizíyah,	Lakhnautí.
637—639	Bahrám Sháh,	Dehlí.
639—644	Mas'úd,	Dehlí.
644—664	Mahmúd I.,	Dehlí.
664—686	Balban,	Dehlí.
686—689	Kai-Kubád,	Dehlí.
689—695	Fíróz II.,	Dehlí.
695	Ibráhím I.,	Dehlí.
695—715	Muhammad Sháh I.,	Dehlí, *Deógír*.
716—720	Mubárak I.,	Dehlí, *Kutbábád* (i.e. Dehlí ?).
720	Khusrú,	Dehlí.
720—725	Taghlak I.,	Dehlí, Deógír, TALANG.
725—752	Muhammad ibn Taghlak,	Dehlí, Satgáon, *Sonárgáon*, Agrah, Taghlakpúr (i.e. Tirhút ?), Daulatábád and Deógír, Sultánpúr, (i.e. Warangol,) Lakhnautí (i.e. Gaur).

* Mints in the National Collection are printed in roman letters; those from Mr. Thomas's *Chronicles*, in italics; while those from Mr. Rodgers' papers are printed in small capitals.

752—790	Fíróz III.,	Dehlí.
790—791	Taghlak II.,	Dehlí.
792—795	Muhammad III.,	Dehlí.
795	Sikandar I.,	Dehlí.
795—797	Mahmúd II.,	Dehlí.
797—802	Nasrat,	Dehlí.
824—837	Mubárak II.,	Dehlí.
837—847	Muhammad IV.,	Dehlí.
847—855	'Álim,	Dehlí.
855—894	Buhlól,	Dehlí, Jaunpúr.
894—923	Sikandar II.,	*Dehlí.*
923—930	Ibráhím II.,	
946—952	Shér Sháh,	Dehlí (Jahánpanáh), Sharífábád, Shérgarh, Agrah, Gwalior, Shérgadah, Kálpí, Hisár, *Rantambhór, Chunár, Biáná, Nárnól, Bhánpúr,* SAMBHAL, ALWÁR, UJAIN.
952—960	Islám Sháh,	Agrah, Gwalior, Satgáon, *Shakk-i-Bakar, Sharífábád, Shérgarh.*
960—961	Muhammad 'Ádil,	Nárnól, *Gwalior.*

Some of these mints have prefixes. Dehlí is generally adorned with the epithet حضرة; but sometimes دار الملك is substituted, and rarely تخت گاه. The last appellation is also given to Daulatábad; اقليم is prefixed to Taghlakpúr, ساهه to Jaunpúr, قلعة to Deógír, and بلدة or بلد to Ghazní.

Some mints have double names: e.g., دار الاسلام or دار الخلافة, or جهانپناه, or قطباباد, stands for Dehlí; ديوگير and دولتاباد are synonymous; whilst سلطانپور represents Warangol, and تغلقپور probably for Tirhút. The appearance of Jaunpúr as the second mint of Buhlól is interesting when it is recollected that it was this Sultán who re-annexed Jaunpúr in 893 after it had been independent for a century.

It will be noticed that the names of several of the Sultáns are absent from the preceding table. This is owing to various causes; Aibek, for instance, is not known to have struck any coins at all; Abu-Bakr, Sikandar II., Ibráhím II., etc., issued coins without stating the names of the mints; while Daulat Khán Lódí and Khizr Khán, in the general confusion which accompanied the invasion of India by Tímúr, preferred rather to trade upon the traditional credit of their predecessors than to make any demands upon the people's trust in their personal solvency, and thus issued their coins in the name of Fíróz III. or Muhammad III., the mints of which issues cannot be held to offer very trustworthy evidence of the extent of their strikers' dominion, which, however, we know from other sources to have been limited to a small district immediately surrounding Dehlí. Neither of these two puppets was a king in any real sense, and to such, "it mattered little whose superscription was placed on the public money,—his duty was confined to authorising the legality of the new issues by so much of his attestation as was implied in the annual date recorded on the reverse, . . . a system, indeed, which the East India Company, of their own free will, imitated with much credit and simplicity by striking their rupees in the name of Sháh 'Álam and other defunct monarchs of Dehlí, whose money had of old obtained good repute in the local bázárs. But as the progressive annual dates, which were needed to test the good faith of Oriental princes, came in process of time to be a source of confusion and an opportunity for money-changers, the Government adopted the expedient of selecting the best current coin of the day, and based their standard upon its intrinsic value; and so the immutable date of 'the XIX *san* (year) of Sháh 'Álam' came to figure upon our much-prized 'Sicca Rupees.'"*

The chief importance of the coinage of the Sultáns of Dehlí lies in its bearing upon the currencies of India. It is before all things a series which attracts the metrologist. Any one who has studied Mr. Thomas's elaborate examination of the relations between these issues and the ancient Indian metric system will understand the value of the coinage of Dehlí in this respect. I do not propose to recapitulate here the results of Mr. Thomas's researches, which are easily accessible in his *Chronicles;* but a sketch of the principal developments of the coinage is necessary to a due appreciation of the various pieces described in the following pages.

In considering the general character of the Dehlí series, we must set aside the introductory issues of Muhammad ibn Sám and his lieutenant Yildiz, which are not only of very uncertain weights, but obviously indicate an attempt to carry on the Muhammadan system of large dirhams. The conqueror of Hindústán readily recognized the fact that it was not to such issues that he must resort in his dealings with his new Indian subjects. From time immemorial the staple of the currency in the northern provinces of India had consisted of small copper and *billon* (silver and copper) pieces, which later on came to be known from the locality as *Dehliwáls*. These, stamped with the traditional religious emblems, the Bull of Siva and the Kábul or Chohán horseman, would inevitably form the models upon which an adapted coinage must be based, if it were to obtain favour in the eyes of a conservative people. Accordingly, Muhammad ibn Sám issued Dehliwáls, with these emblems and his own name inscribed in Nágarí or Hindí characters

* E. Thomas: *Chronicles*, pp. 329, 330; *International Numismata Orientalia*, vol i, part 1, *Ancient Indian Weights*, p. 53 *f.*

of a rude type. So closely did he imitate the style of the preceding local coinage, or so scrupulously did he avail himself of the services of the old moneyers, that it has been found possible to attribute many of his coins to mints whose names are not recorded upon their surfaces, by indications of style and treatment of the devices. Similar reasons induced him to preserve, though only for a short time, the peculiar gold issues of Kanauj, with a rude figure of the goddess Lakhshmí, adding his name in Nágarí. The billon Dehliwáls, which for convenience are headed "Copper" in the present volume, retained their old important position in the currency of Hindústán through the greater part of the duration of the dynasty founded by Muhammad ibn Sám. They underwent various modifications, especially in the substitution of Arabic for Nágarí inscriptions; and there are minor differences in the form and position of the Bull Nandí and the Horseman, which have been noted. But the main fact, that a billon currency formed the staple of exchange in Hindústán, is undisturbed. Muhammad ibn Sám's conquests "were always associated with an adaptation, more or less complete, of the local currency; hence we find the peculiar type of the Ghóri Horseman retained in its own locality; the distinctive Kurmán outline [upright posture] of the Bull of Siva maintains its identity through succeeding foreign dynasties; . . . Ajmír, Dehlí, Multán, and Sind, each preserved, but little modified, a Tughra outline of the early device of the first Brahman Kings of Kábul,—the Cavalier with the reverse of the Sacred Bull."*

Side by side with this native coinage, a new and characteristic issue was introduced by Altamsh in the early part of the seventh century of the Flight. This was the silver

* E. Thomas: *Chronicles*, p. 36.

Tankah, which held its place as the standard silver coin to the end of the dynasty, and was so much approved that a gold Tankah, of equal weight, was added by Balban in the same century, which retained its position, with a brief interruption, for more than a century,—until, in fact, the precarious tenure of power by the Sultáns of Dehlí rendered any issue of gold coins incompatible with the state of the treasury. The Tankah, silver or gold, should weigh 175 grains, and the existing specimens bear out the estimate with tolerable accuracy. Seventy-five silver Tankahs in the British Museum, from Altamsh to Taghlak Sháh I., weigh collectively 12,550 grains, or a trifle over 166 grains apiece, which, allowing for wear and sweating, is a fair average. None of these 75 pieces fall below 161 (indeed only two fall below 163 grains), and some reach the weight of 171. The gold show an even better average, for 21 specimens in the British Museum, from Balban to Taghlak Sháh I., weigh collectively 3526 grs., which gives $167\frac{19}{21}$ as the weight of each, or just under 168 grs. One of these goes as high as 173, and only one falls below 164. Thus from the beginning of a regular silver coinage under Altamsh, about the year 632 of the Hijrah, to the time of Muhammad ibn Taghlak, A.H. 725, the Tankah was the standard of currency in the empire of Dehlí.

With Muhammad ibn Taghlak begins a series of innovations, which, although they were not destined to last long, introduced in their brief duration many curious and novel features into the currency of Hindústán. Muhammad Sháh is stated to have had some such change in contemplation with regard to the Tankah as Muhammad ibn Taghlak eventually carried into effect. He was anxious to strike a new Tankah of 140 grains, in order to pay his Sipáhís, or Sepoys, with as little expense as possible. This was the precise reduction which Ibn Taghlak effected. His new

'Adlis, or "equitable [coins]," as they were called,* for no very obvious reason, weighed 140 grains, and from A.H. 725 to 730 the new standard obtained throughout his empire. The British Museum specimens range from 137 to 151 grs., and give an average of 141 grs. In A.H. 730, however, Muhammad ibn Taghlak thought better of his reform, and other coins of that year maintain the old weight of 169 (for 175) grs. Simultaneously he had attempted an alteration in the standard of the gold Tankahs, which he raised to 200 grs., as witness the pieces of 197, 198, and 199 grs. in this volume. But this change was even more short-lived than that in the silver; it began in A.H. 726, and already in 729 and 730 the old Tankah of 175 grs. is again represented by gold pieces weighing 168, 169, and 171 grs.

But the most remarkable of all Muhammad ibn Taghlak's monetary enterprises was the attempt to introduce a forced currency of brass at the value of the Tankah. Such attempts at a fiduciary coinage had before been made by Oriental sovereigns. Khubilai Khán, the Mongol emperor of China, had succeeded in perfecting a very convenient paper currency in the Celestial empire; and the Mongol Ilkhán of Persia, Gai-khatu, with very different motives, had endeavoured to force a paper money upon his Persian subjects; but the strenuous resistence he encountered made an end of the fraud and of his own sovereignty. Muhammad ibn Taghlak's forced currency was of a different order. It was chiefly of brass, and the state of the treasury seems to have justified any system of nominal values, inasmuch as Ibn Taghlak could easily have redeemed the whole issue at the nominal prices. Indeed, when, after about three years, (730—732,) the trial proved unsuccessful, in consequence of innumerable imitations, against which the Sultán had organized no regal protective marks, Muhammad ibn Taghlak

* The name occurs on the coinage itself.

took up the whole brass currency, genuine and forged alike, at the values for which they were intended to pass. In such circumstances there can be no question of dishonesty on the part of the ruler. That he anticipated some reluctance on the part of his subjects to accept the brass currency as equivalent to the silver Tankah may be seen from the character of the legends with which the new coins were inscribed :—من اطاع السلطان فقد اطاع الرحمن " Whoso obeys the Sultán obeys the Compassionate ;" اطيعوا الله واطيعوا الرسول واولى الامر منكم لا يولا السلطان كل الناس بعضهم بعضا "Obey God and obey the Prophet, and those in authority among you : sovereignty is not conferred upon all men ; some of them (precede) others ;" etc. At the same time, while thus appealing to the Korán for the inculcation of obedience to the powers that be, Muhammad ibn Taghlak was careful to let the people understand for exactly how much the new piece was intended to pass. Thus we find the inscription مهر شد تنكة رائج در روزگار بنده اميدوار محمد تغلق " Sealed as a Tankah current in the reign of the slave hopeful [of grace] Muhammad [ibn] Taghlak," and again مهر شد تنكة پنجاه كانى در روزگار الخ " Sealed as a Tankah of fifty Kánis," or Gánis, etc. ; or ضرب الربعى " Struck [as] the fourth ; الدرهم الشرعى "The legal dirham," النصفى " The half-piece ;" عدل هشت كانى " Good [for] eight Kánis," or سكة دو كانى " Money of two Kánis," and finally چيتل امانى يكانى " A Chítal equal to one Káni :" but these varieties are not all represented in the National Collection. In Mr. Thomas's No. 201, I read سكة not تنكة.

In order to understand what these denominations mean, we must consult Mr. Thomas's * table of the Currency during the reign of Muhammad ibn Taghlak, here subjoined with some modifications in the arrangement.

* *Chronicles*, p. 219.

MUHAMMAD IBN TAGHLAK'S CURRENCY.

	Káni.	Du-káni.	Shash-káni.	Hasht-kani.	Duwáz-dah-k.	Shánz-dah-k.	Tankah.
Káni (or Chítal),	1						
Du-káni (or Sultání)	2	1					
Shash-káni . .	6	3	1				
Hasht-káni . .	8	4	$1\frac{1}{3}$	1			
Duwázdah-káni .	12	6	2	$1\frac{1}{2}$	1		
Shánzdah-káni .	16	8	$2\frac{2}{3}$	2	$1\frac{1}{3}$	1	
Tankah (*old*, 175 grs.) . .	64	32	$10\frac{2}{3}$	8	$5\frac{1}{3}$	4	1

The ancient quaternary scale is here observable throughout: there are no fives or tens. The new *'Adlí* Tankah of 140 grs., however, correspond to 50 Kánis, and pieces of 25 Kánis were struck to subdivide it. Afterwards Fíróz Sháh III. appears to have introduced 2, 10, 24, and 48 Káni pieces.

On comparing the weights of the forced brass currency with the foregoing table, many difficulties present themselves. Mr. Thomas once seemed inclined to fix the denomination (only tentatively, it is true,) by the weights of the pieces described in his *Chronicles*. I am disposed to think that the weight had very little to do with the distinction of denominations. The brass coin intended to pass for a silver Tankah, and bearing an inscription stating so, does indeed carry a weight of 136 grs., nearly approaching the 140 grs. of the new 'Adlí Tankah, which, however, at the time of the forced currency, seems to have already been abolished in favour of the old 175 grs. Tankah, so that we should rather expect the brass coin to weigh 175 grs. But even if it were granted that the 140 Tankah is intended to be represented in weight by the brass pieces in question, the subdivisions show no correspondence in the matter of weight.

The piece marked 8 Kánis weighs 53 grs., which is neither an eighth part of 136 nor a 6¼ part, taking the two values of the old and new Tankahs (64 and 50 Kánis) into consideration. If the 136 brass Tankah is meant to equal 50 Kánis, the 8 Káni piece should weigh about 21 grs. Or if the brass Tankah of 136 grs. is intended to represent the old Tankah of 175 grs., the 8 Káni piece should follow a similar reduction in weight, and should hardly exceed 17 grs. Again, on whatever principle we accommodate the 8 Káni piece to the Tankah, it is impossible to give a satisfactory account, on the weight system, of the Du-káṇi piece, which weighs 25 grs., instead of 13, as it should if it is to bear any relation to the 8 Káni piece. Then there is a unique *Chítal* of copper, equal to 1 Káni, but weighing no less than 74 grs., which must upset all calculations. Nor is it easy, on the principle of a uniform scale of weights, to explain the pieces of 112 and 55 grs., which Mr. Thomas suggests may be 40 and 20 Kánis. Why should a 20 Káni piece weigh only 2 grs. more than an 8 Káni piece? A remarkable *Dirham Shar'í*, "Legal dirham," also appears in the series, which comes up to 80 grs., which no legal dirham ever did; while the *Nisfy* or half-dirham, (as Mr. Thomas terms it,) weighs no less than 103 grs.

I do not quote these weights under any impression that Mr. Thomas has ever sought to prove that the brass coinage was strictly adjusted to a regular scale of weights corresponding to those of the silver coins they were intended to supplant; indeed a remark of his (on p. 248) shows that he is perfectly alive to the discrepancies in the scale of weights; but I am anxious to state clearly that any deduction from the weights is likely to be fallacious, inasmuch as the closest examination reveals no system or graduated scale whatever. The lower denominations were lighter than the higher, and that is, I believe, all that can be formulated about them on the subject.

Another curious feature in the currency—not the forced issues—of this "Prince of Moneyers" is the striking of gold and copper coins in the sole name of the contemporary Khalífah of Egypt, the *fainéant* representative of the once powerful house of 'Abbás. The only parallel instance in the Dehlí series is the remarkable coin of Altamsh, No. 35, where only the Khalífah Al-Mustansir's name appears in the inscriptions.* From the earliest issues of the Sultáns of Dehlí, the spiritual lords of the Muslims were never neglected. Muhammad ibn Sám put the name of the reigning Khalífah of the yet surviving dynasty of Baghdád upon his silver coins, while the Nágarí letters सी हमीरः, *Srí Hamírah*, may perhaps stand for امير المؤمنين *Amir al-mu-minín*, as the occurrence in the same position of the form सी षलीफ, *Srí Shalípha*, i.e. *Al-Khalífah*, seems to show; though *Srí Hamírah* might of course equally well represent *Al-Amír* simply, and refer to Muhammad ibn Sám himself. From the time of Muhammad ibn Sám to that of Fíróz II., the names of the 'Abbásí Khalífahs of Baghdád appear regularly on the gold and silver coins; and even so late as 695, forty years after the forcible destruction of the Baghdád Khalifate and the murder of Al-Musta'sim by Húlágú, the name of this ill-fated Pontiff is seen on the coinage of Dehlí. At last, however, the Sultáns of Hindústán seem to have realized that there could be little spiritual benefit in retaining the name of a Khalífah who had been dead for forty years, and accordingly from the accession of Ibráhím I. the coinage does not record the name of the Khalífah, but inscribes only a bare reference to his existence, in the Sultán's title *Násir Amír-al-mu-minín*, to which Muhammad I. added the title of *Yamín al-Khiláfah*.

The next alteration took place under Mubárak Sháh I.,

* E. Thomas, *Chronicles*, p. 46.

who, after beginning with the stereotyped *Násir Amír-al-mu-minín* of his predecessors, assumed the dignity of Khalífah himself, in the style الواثق بالله أمير المؤمنين, in 717, adding such other improvements as خليفة الله, خليفة رب العالمين and terming Dehlí the "Abode of the Khalifate," Dár al-Khiláfah. Khusrú Sháh styled himself ولّى أمير المؤمنين, and Taghlak Sháh I. returned to the old form of Násir Amír-al-mu-minín. Then his son Muhammad introduced the crowning acknowledgment of the Egyptian Khalifate when he struck coins in which he omitted all mention of himself, and substituted the inscription "This Khalífatí dínár was struck . . . in the time of the Imám Al-Mustakfí," the then reigning 'Abbásí Khalífah of the restored line in Egypt. It was not apparently until this period, more than eighty years after the revival of the Khalifate in Egypt under the Mamlúks, that the Sultáns of Dehlí became aware of this restoration; and Muhammad ibn Taghlak certainly spared no pains to emphasize the discovery. After his brief issue of purely "Khalífatí" coins, in gold and copper, in the middle of the eighth century of the Flight, the name of the reigning Egyptian Khalífah appears regularly upon the Dehlí mintings, in conjunction with that of the Sultán, until A.H. 795; after which year the monarchs of Dehlí seem again to have become uncertain as to the names of the successive Khalífahs, and therefore contented themselves with simply inscribing the fact that there was a Khalífah of some name or another, without seeking to indicate his precise titles. The forms, "In the time of the Prince of the Faithful," فى زمن أمير المؤمنين, or "The Khalífah [is] the Prince of the Faithful," retained their place on the coinage until the time of Shér Sháh, with the variation of *Náïb Amír-al-mu-minín*. Shér Sháh abolished the style of Khalífah altogether from the coinage, with a due sense of historical accuracy, since the Egyptian Khalifate had by then been absorbed by the Sultáns of Turkey, and the Sultán of Dehlí could not be expected to understand that the spiritual power thus transferred ought to be recognised in so remote a region as Hindustán. Shér Sháh, however, upheld the character of the Dehlí coinage for Sunní orthodoxy by inserting the names and epithets of the first four Khalífahs, Abu-Bakr, 'Umar, 'Uthmán, and 'Alí, and the example was followed by his successors to the close of the dynasty.

After the reign of Muhammad ibn Taghlak the coinage of the Sultáns of Dehlí greatly deteriorates. Only eight gold Tankahs are found in the British Museum collection after this monarch, and of these but one is later than Fíróz III., his immediate successor. The specimens in question are of the old weight of 167 to 170 grs. The silver also becomes greatly diminished. With the exception of a few posthumous silver Tankahs, struck chiefly by Khizr Khán in the name of Muhammad III., about 817, no silver coins occur in the British Museum between the death of Muhammad ibn Taghlak and the accession of Shér Sháh, an interval of nearly 200 years. Shér Sháh and his successors abolished the *billon* coinage, which had absorbed almost all the exchange of India, and restored the silver Tankah in its original weight of about 175 grs. The specimens in the Museum fall little below this figure.

The inscriptions on the coins of the Sultáns are unusually monotonous. Save in the phenomenal issues of Muhammad ibn Taghlak, the religious inscriptions are of the commonest order, and there are not many even of these. A few peculiar forms may be noticed: e.g., the complete form of the Profession of Faith اشهد ان لا اله الا الله الخ on 260—263; والله الغنى وانتم الفقرا (Kur. xxxv. 15); اطيعوا الله واطيعوا الرسول واولى الامر منكم لا يولا السطان كل الناس بعضكم بعضا (partly from Kur. iv. 62); and the benedictory formulas اعلى اجره, انار الله برهانه, and جل الله ظلاله وجلاله. The titles of the sovereigns of Dehlí are as monotonous as their religious legends. They are all "Sultáns," and, after Bahrám, "Sháhs" also, and the almost universal epithet they add to exalt the former title is الاعظم. Down to the time of Muhammad ibn Taghlak, they hardly ever varied this formula, although Muhammad ibn Sám himself, when under his brother's suzerainty, began with the variety of المعظم. Original in his titles, as in everything else, Muhammad ibn Taghlak abandoned the cherished epithet, which Taghlak I. had already shaken by his occasional substitution of the epithet الغازى. Muhammad his son began his gold coinage with a posthumous coin in memory of his father, bearing the unprecedented series السعيد الشهيد الغازى. This he followed by various new titles, such as السلطان العادل, العبد الراجى رحمة الله, الواثق بتائيد الرحمن الراجى رحمة الله الكريم, المجاهد فى سبيل الله, and the Persian بنده اميدوار, representing the Arabic العبد الراجى. After his time, the old formula returns once or twice, chiefly on posthumous issues in the name of Muhammad III.; but as a rule the later Sultáns of Dehlí were satisfied with the simple epithet, inaugurated by Fíróz II. (who also styled himself الواثق بتائيد يزدانى) of سلطانى, *Sultání* or *As-Sultání*, with "Lieutenant of the Prince of the Faithful," نائب امير المؤمنين, not unfrequently added. The Lódís abolished this title and called themselves المتوكل على الرحمن; and Shér Sháh and Islám Sháh adopted the style of السلطان العادل; or, on the copper issues, the very peculiar formula الامير الحامى الدين الدنان (or الحاكمى). Added to the first title are generally a *lakab*, such as Násir-ad-dín, and a *kunyah*, which is universally *Abu-l-Muzaffar*, whenever there is a kunyah at all, except in two cases when it is *Abu-l-Mujáhid*. Násir Amír-al-mu-minín is, as has been said, a common addition to these titles, from Altamsh to Muhammad I., and on the coins of Taghlak I. "Sword of the Prince of the Faithful," سيف أمير المؤمنين, occurs on the coinage of

Fíróz II., as does the form نائب أمير المؤمنين, which remains in use to the time of Mubárak II. The one Queen of the line, Riziyah ibnat Altamsh, used the form نصرة أمير المؤمنين. So at least the specimen in the British Museum reads, and this is confirmed by a specimen described and engraved by Dr. Hoernle in the *Journal* of the Bengal Asiatic Society (1881). Mr. Thomas has read مهرة أمير المؤمنين from another example. The only other titles of importance occurring on the coins under review are those of Muhammad I., اسكندر الثانى يمين الخلافة; of Mubarak I., اسكندر الزمان, يمين الخلافة, soon changing to الامام الاعظم . . . الواثق بالله امير المومنين, and Khusrú Sháh's الواثق بنصر الرحمن ولى امير المومنين, where Mr. Thomas has read الواثق بخير . . ., which is not confirmed by any specimen in the British Museum.

The orthography of the name "Altamsh" demands a few words. I have followed Mr. Thomas in retaining the most usual spelling: but there can be no doubt that it is not the most accurate representation of the original Túrkí, whatever the meaning of that original may have been. There is generally a single stroke after the ت, and not infrequently another before the ل: so that the complete form would seem to be ايلتتمش *Íl-tutmish.* The Nagarí transcript लितितिमिसि *Lititimisi* agrees tolerably well with this restoration; and the meaning of Íl-tutmish, 'Hand-grasper,' 'Supporter,' 'Upholder,' is sufficiently appropriate. Mr. Redhouse, however, on the authority of Ahmad Wafík Páshá, suggests an alternative reading in ايلتيمش, from ايلتماك, 'to convey,' 'carry off,' *i.e.*, 'the kidnapped,' or slave who was 'carried off:' and adds that it might also be taken in the active sense, as meaning the 'carrier off' or ravisher (of the heart).

There are many points that might here be raised with regard to the origin and localization of the Brahmanical emblems and symbols, and the peculiarities of Nagarí palæography as exhibited on the coins: but these will more appropriately be considered in the volume of the Indian Catalogue which will treat exclusively of the Hindú coinages.

I have already indicated two or three small matters in which I have been compelled reluctantly to differ from the opinion of Mr. Thomas, and it is necessary to enumerate a few more such minor differences. When there is merely a question as to how much of an undisputed inscription is legible, I shall not here discuss what is only an affair of eyes and microscopes. The rejection from the present volume of Mr. Thomas's No. 7 requires, however, some explanation, inasmuch as the coin exists in the British Museum. I reject it, because I am convinced that it is not a coin of Muhammad ibn Sám at all, but of one of the Ghaznawís, probably Khusrú Malik. The fabric alone, I think, shows it is no fellow to the issues of Muhammad ibn Sám, and the inscription, as I read it, confirms the rejection. No. 120 of the *Chronicles*, which is the same coin as No. 138 of the present volume, bears, according to Mr. Thomas, the date 680, which he adds is "clearly an error," with which I must concur, since I can only make it 695. Mr. Thomas's No. 121 presents a slight displacement of the inscriptions in the *Chronicles*, for the word امير should be in the middle line. In his No. 146, Mr. Thomas reads Dár-al-Khiláfah, where I find Dár-al-Mulk, but the two may not be of precisely the same issue. On the coins described under No. 297 by Mr. Thomas, I can find no distinct trace of the mint-name he gives. On p. 51 of this catalogue will be found a foot-note in which I venture to dissent from Mr. Thomas's reading of a posthumous coin of Taghlak I. The rejection of the presumed date on the reverse at once removes Mr. Thomas's No. 158 to the side of his No. 178, as a posthumous, and not as he supposed a contemporary, issue of that Sultán. The title *Ash-Shahíd* alone is, I think, enough to prove that Taghlak was dead when the coin was struck, for I cannot recall an instance of so very significant a title being assumed by a living king.

I may add, in reference to No. 73 in this volume, that I can find no trace of the بالله and محمد Dr. Hoernle refers to in the *Journal* of the Bengal Asiatic Society (1881).

In the arrangement of posthumous coins, as well as in some other minor details of order, I have departed from the pattern which is set, generally with excellent judgment, in the *Chronicles*. I class the posthumous coins under the king whose name they bear, and give a cross-reference in the place where they should come if the order were strictly chronological. The matter is merely a question of convenience; and I found that the coins were more clearly described and more easily compared in this order than if they had been placed where their dates demanded. Instances of this arrangement will be frequently met with in this volume, and the student must not be deceived by the classification into the belief that the Sultáns enjoyed preternaturally long reigns. By a contrary principle to that which prompted the issue of posthumous coins, Nos. 410—412 in this catalogue were struck by Muhammad III. before he actually became Sultán, when he was associated with his father Fíróz III. in the government. It would have been better if I had indicated this circumstance in the heading.

As coins, without reference to their historical or geographical or other relations, those of the Sultáns of Dehlí are singularly fine. Especially beautiful are the clear-cut gold issues of Muhammad ibn Taghlak, where the smaller superficies enabled a better impression to be struck with the die. But the chief test of a coinage is rather in the assay than in the calligraphy, though the latter is not to be despised upon Muhammadan coins, where the finer departments of the engraver's art could not be allowed free scope. Mr. Thomas has given some details of assaying experiments with the coins of Dehlí, and the result in the higher metals shows great regularity. Muhammad I.'s gold, for example, had a fineness of 94·2, and Fíróz II.'s of 94·5.

More interesting are the assays which Mr. Thomas had

made in India of the billon coinage, by the usual native process of blowing off the copper with lead. The following are some of his results :—

Twelve of Nasír-ad-dín Mahmúd's *dehliwáls*, with a collective weight of 584 grs., produced 149 grs. of silver, or 12·14 (nearly ¼th) apiece.

Various specimens of Fíróz III., (*Chronicles*, No. 228), weighing from 131·5 to 141 grs. each, contained irregular proportions of silver, ranging from 12 to 24 grs. apiece.

Four coins of Buhlól Lódí, weighing about 140 grs. each, gave 0 gr., 15·3 grs., 14 grs., and 6·7 grs., silver.

The average silver in the coins of Sikandar ibn Buhlól, from an assay of over thirty, was 5·64 in each piece, of an average weight of about 140 grs. each.

The subjoined tables of the genealogical relations of the various princes whose money is described in this volume, together with the map of mediæval India, will be useful to the student of this dynasty in its connection with the history of India at large.

In conclusion, I am glad to have this opportunity of expressing my thanks to Mr. Edward Thomas, not only for the assistance which every student of the coins of the Sultáns of Dehlí must derive from his learned and exhaustive *Chronicles*, but also for the kindness with which he has permitted me to examine his own annotated copy of that work, and has read the proof-sheets of this Introduction. I am also much indebted to Professor Percy Gardner for his supervision of the Nágarí inscriptions included in this volume, to Mr. Redhouse, Dr. Stickel, and MM. Tiesenhausen and Sauvaire, for various suggestions ; while to the Keeper of Coins, in his minute and scrupulous revision of every line of the work, I owe many valuable corrections and improvements.

STANLEY LANE-POOLE.

Richmond, Nov. 24, 1884.

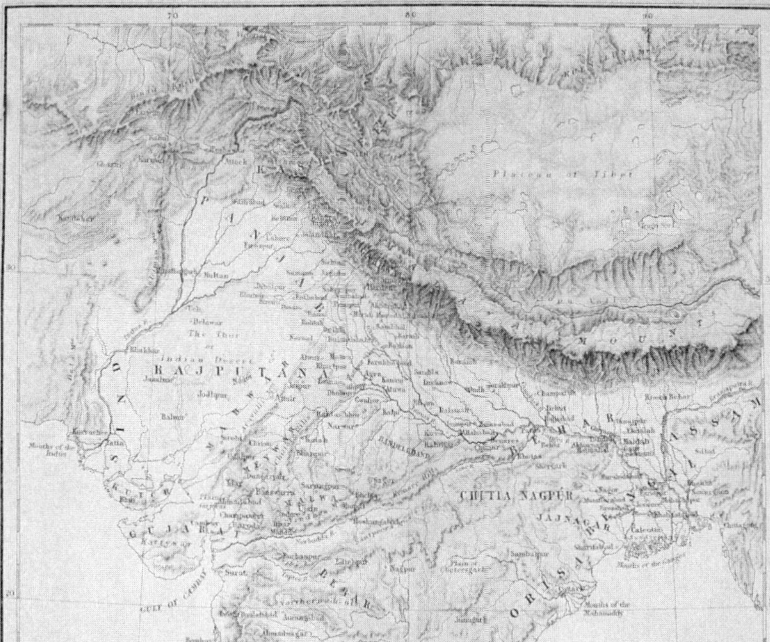
MEDIAEVAL INDIA
ILLUSTRATING THE
MINTS
OF THE
MUHAMMADAN RULERS
Scale of Miles
ARABIAN SEA
BAY OF BENGAL
Plateau of Tibet
RAJPUTANA
DEKHAN
TILANGANA
CHUTIA NAGPUR
JAJNAGAR
GUJARAT
MALWA
ORISSA
ASSAM
CEYLON
Laccadive Islands
Maldive Islands
GULF OF CAMBAY
Longitude East of Greenwich
70
80
90
30
20
10

GENEALOGICAL TREES OF THE SULTÁNS OF DEHLÍ.

I. FIRST DYNASTY.

- 1. Mu'izz-ad-dín Muhammad Ghórí
  - 2. Kutb-ad-dín Aibak
    - 3. Árám Sháh
    - *daughter* = 4. Altamsh
      - 5. Rukn-ad-dín Fíróz Sháh I.
        - 8. 'Alá-ad-dín Mas'úd Sháh
      - 6. Rizíyah
      - Mahmúd (*Bengal*)
      - 7. Mu'izz-ad-dín Bahrám Sháh
      - 9. Násir-ad-dín Mahmúd Sháh I.
      - *daughter* = 10. Ghiyás-ad-dín Balban
        - Násir-ad-dín Bughrá Khán (*Bengal*)
          - 11. Mu'izz-ad-dín Kai-Kubád
          - Kai-Káús (*Bengal*)
          - Fíróz Sháh (*Bengal*)
            - Bughrá Sháh (*Bengal*)
            - Násir-ad-dín (*Lakhnautí*)
            - Bahádur Sháh (*E. Bengal*)
              - Muhammad
            - Kutlú Khán
            - Hátim Khán (*Bihár*)

*** ... Dotted lines signify the relation of master and slave.

II. SECOND DYNASTY.

12. Jalál-ad-dín Fíróz Sháh II. *Khalji*

brother

13. Rukn-ad-dín Ibráhím Sháh

14. 'Alá-ad-dín Muhammad Sháh I.

15. Shiháb-ad-dín 'Umar Sháh

16. Kutb-ad-dín Mubárak Sháh I.

17. Násir-ad-dín Khusrú (*slave vizír*)

III. THIRD DYNASTY.

- 18. Ghiyás-ad-dín Taghlak Sháh I.
  - 19. Muhammad (Ulugh Khán Júná)
    - Mahmúd
- Sipáh-Sálár Rajab
  - 20. Fíróz Sháh III.
    - Fath
      - 21. Ghiyás-ad-dín Taghlak Sháh II.
      - 26. Nasrat Sháh
    - Zafar
      - 22. Abú-Bakr Sháh
    - 23. Muhammad Sháh III.
      - 24. Sikandar Sháh I.
      - 25. Mahmúd Sháh II.

IV. FOURTH DYNASTY.

28. Khizr Khán *Sayyid*

29. Mubárak Sháh II.

Faríd

30. Muhammad Sháh IV.

31. 'Álim Sháh

V. FIFTH DYNASTY.

32. Buhlól *Lódí*

33. Sikandar II.

34. Ibráhím II.

VI. SIXTH DYNASTY.

- 35. Faríd-ad-dín Shér Sháh
  - 36. Islám Sháh
    - Fíróz Khán
- *brother*
  - 37. Muhammad 'Ádil Sháh
    - Shér Khán
- Ghází Khán Súr
  - 38. Ibráhím Súr
- 39. Sikandar Sháh III.

TABLE

OF THE

METHOD OF TRANSLITERATION ADOPTED IN THIS CATALOGUE.

أ	*a*	ظ	*z*
ب	*b*	ع	'
پ	*p*	غ	*gh*
ت	*t*	ف	*f*
ث	*s*	ق	*k*
ج	*j*	ك	*k*
چ	*ch*	گ	*g*
ح	*h*	ل	*l*
خ	*kh*	م	*m*
د	*d*	ن	*n*
ذ	*z*	ه	*h*
ر	*r*	و	*w*
ز	*z*	ی	*y*
س	*s*	َ *a*	ـَا *á*
ش	*sh*	ِ *i*	ـِی *í*
ص	*s*	ُ *u*	ـُو *ú*
ض	*z*	ـَی *ai, é*	ـَو *au, ó*
ط	*t*		

CONTENTS.

f

ERRATA.

P. 18, *for* اليتمش *read* التتمش.

P. 33, no. 135 *delete* Pl. III.

P. 47, no. 226, *delete* Pl. IV.

P. 93, *for* فرسد *read* فريد.

P. 111, *for* سير *read* شير.

The following references to the Plates have been accidentally omitted :—

Nos. 268, 274, 276, 284, 309, 323, are figured in Plate V.; and nos. 518 and 530 in Plate VIII.

THE SULTÁNS OF DEHLÍ.

THE SULTÁNS OF DEHLÍ.

FIRST DYNASTY.—TURKS.

		A.H.	A.D.
I.	Mu'izz-ad-dín Muhammad ibn Sám . .	589	1193
II.	Kutb-ad-dín Aibak	602	1205
III.	Árám Sháh	607	1210
IV.	Shams-ad-dín Altamsh	607	1210
V.	Rukn-ad-dín Fíróz Sháh I. . . .	633	1235
VI.	Rizíyah	634	1236
VII.	Mu'izz-ad-dín Bahrám Sháh . . .	637	1239
VIII.	'Alá-ad-dín Mas'úd Sháh . . .	639	1241
IX.	Násir-ad-dín Mahmúd Sháh I. . . .	644	1246
X.	Ghiyás-ad-dín Balban	664	1265
XI.	Mu'izz-ad-dín Kai-Kubád . . .	686	1287

SECOND DYNASTY.—KHALJÍS.

		A.H.	A.D.
XII.	Jalál-ad-dín Fíróz Sháh II. . . .	689	1290
XIII.	Rukn-ad-dín Ibráhím Sháh I. . .	695	1295
XIV.	'Alá-ad-dín Muhammad Sháh I. . .	695	1295
XV.	Shiháb-ad-dín 'Umar Sháh . . .	715	1315
XVI.	Kutb-ad-dín Mubárak Sháh I. . . .	716	1316
XVII.	Násir-ad-dín Khusrú Sháh . . .	720	1320

THIRD DYNASTY.—TAGHLAK SHAHÍS.

		A.H.	A.D.
XVIII.	Ghiyás-ad-dín Taghlak Sháh I. . .	720	1320
XIX.	Muhammad II. ibn Taghlak . .	725	1324
XX.	Fíróz Sháh III.	752	1351
XXI.	Taghlak Sháh II.	790	1388
XXII.	Abu-Bakr Sháh	791	1388
XXIII.	Muhammad Sháh III. . . .	792	1389
XXIV.	Sikandar Sháh I.	795	1392
XXV.	Mahmúd Sháh II.	795	1392
XXVI.	Nasrat Sháh (Interregnum) . . .	797	1394
	Mahmúd restored	802	1399
XXVII.	Daulat Khán Lódí	815	1412

FOURTH DYNASTY.—SEYYIDS.

		A.H.	A.D.
XXVIII.	Khizr Khán	817	1414
XXIX.	Mu'izz-ad-dín Mubárak Sháh II. .	824	1421
XXX.	Muhammad Sháh IV. . . .	837	1433
XXXI.	'Álim Sháh	847	1443

FIFTH DYNASTY.—AFGHANS.

		A.H.	A.D.
XXXII.	Buhlól Lódí	855	1451
XXXIII.	Sikandar II. ibn Buhlól . . .	894	1488
XXXIV.	Ibráhím II. ibn Sikandar . .	923	1517
	Mughals: Bábar and Humáyún .	930	1526

SIXTH DYNASTY.—AFGHANS.

		A.H.	A.D.
XXXV.	Faríd-ad-dín Shér Sháh . . .	946	1539
XXXVI.	Islám Sháh	952	1545
XXXVII.	Muhammad 'Ádil Sháh . . .	960	1552
XXXVIII.	Ibráhím Súr	961	1553
XXXIX.	Sikandar Sháh III.	962	1554
	Mughals: Humáyún, etc. . .	962	1554

I.—MUHAMMAD IBN SÁM.

A.H. 589—602.

A.—IN CONJUNCTION WITH GHIYÁS-AD-DÍN GHÚRÍ.

SILVER.

Æ No.	Mint: Date.	*Inscriptions arranged in concentric circles.*
1	Ghazní 596	Obv., 1st circle, هو الذى ارسل رسوله بالهدى ودين الحق ليظهره على الد[ين كله ولو] كره المشركون 2nd circle, لا اله الا الله محمد رسول الله السلطان الاعظم 3rd circle, غياث الدنيا والدين ابو الفتح Centre, محمد بن سام Rev., 1st circle, ضرب هذا الدرهم فى بلدة غزنة . . . . . . سنة ست وتسعين وخمسن مائة 2nd circle, الناصر لدين الله السلطان المعظم معز 3rd circle, الدنيا والدين ابو المظفر Centre, محمد بن سام PL. I. (Th. 3). Æ 1·25, Wt. 73

Æ No.	Mint: Date.	
2	Ghazní 596	Obv. and Rev., 1st circles and centres as on 1; but بلد for بلدة Obv., 2nd circle, لا اله الا الله الناصر لدين الله ا[لسلطان] الاعظم 3rd circle, غياث الدنيا والدين ابو . . . . . Rev., 2nd circle, محمد رسول الله السطان المعظم معز 3rd circle, [الدني]ا والدين ابو المظفر Pierced. Æ 1·15, Wt. 48
3	*x* [59]8	Obv., within double square, لا اله الا ال[له محمد رسول الله السلطان الاعظم غياث الدنيا والدين ابو الفتح محمد بن سام In segments, outside square, هو الذى ارسل | . . . . . . | ودين الحق ليظ[هره] | على الدين كله Rev., within double square, الناصر لدين الله السلطان المعظم معز الدنيا و الدين ابو المظفر محمد بن سام In segments, outside square, ضرب . . . | . . . . | سنة ثمان و | . . . . Pl. I. Æ 1·1, Wt. 82

COPPER.*

(Dehliwáls.)

Æ No.	Mint : Date.	*Obv.*	*Rev.*
4		Horseman to left, with lance at charge. Inscription illegible.	ال]سلطان ا]لمعظم غياث الد نيا والدين ابو الفتح محمد بن سام Æ ·55
5	[Láhór ? Th.]	السلطان المعظم معز الدنيا و الدين	محمد بن * سام Pl. I. (Th. 7.)† Æ ·55

---

* Small coins of the size and character of 4 and 5 abound in the Patán series. They are very seldom of pure copper, but usually of a mixture of silver and copper, in the proportions stated in various places in Mr. Thomas's *Chronicles*, and in the Introduction to this volume. The general designation of 'copper' has, however, been adhered to throughout, inasmuch as that metal always predominates.

† The title المعظم seems to indicate that Muhammad was still the lieutenant of his brother غياث الدين ; after whose death, he adopts the form الاعظم.

B.—ALONE.

AV

GOLD.

No.	Mint: Date.	
6	Ghazní 602	Obv., within double square, لا اله الا الله محمد رسول الله الناصر لدين الله امير المومنين In segments, outside square, هو الذى ارسل | رسوله بالهدى | و .... | .... Rev., within double square, السلطان الاعظم معز الدنيا و الدين ابو المظفر محمد بن سام In segments outside square, ضرب هذا | الدينار ببلدة | غزنة فى شهور سنة | اثنى وست مائة Pl. I. AV 1·35, Wt. 322
7	Ghazní 603	Same: but rev. margin ends غزنة فى شهور | سنة ثلث وست مائة and obv. margin is nearly complete to كله (Th. 20.) AV 1·05, Wt. 89

AV No.	Mint: Date.	
8	Ghazní 604	Same: but rev. margin, ضرب هذا | الدينار ببلدة غز[نة] | فى شهور سنة | اربع وست مائة and obv. margin differently distributed. AV 1·35, Wt. 146 The last two coins were probably issued by Yildiz, as Muhammad ibn Sám died in 602. Cf. no. 20.

COPPER.

Æ		Obv.	Rev.
9	[Sind. Th.]	Chohán Horseman to right; on horse's quarter ∵ around, श्री हंमीरः *Srí Hammírah.*	[ا]لسلطان [ا]لاعظم محمد بن سام Pl. I. (Th. 5.) Æ ·6
10, 11		Horseman to left with lance at charge.	Same. Pl. I. (Th. 6.) Æ ·6 Æ ·6
12—16	[Dehlí. Th.]	Chohán Horseman as 9, same inscription, but characters of quite a different style.	The Bull Nandí to left, recumbent: on *Jhul* ل; on side ı. श्री महमद सामे *Srí Mahamad Sáme.* Pl. I. (Th. 10.) Æ ·6 Æ ·6 Æ ·55 Æ ·6 (no sign on side) Æ ·65

Æ No.	Mint: Date.	*Obv.*	*Rev.*
17—19		Similar: but horseman debased, and inscription scarcely traceable.	Similar: but bull debased; inscription in straight line above, स्री महमद स . . Pl. I. (Th. 11.) Æ ·6 Æ ·65 Æ ·65

ISSUES OF TÁJ-AD-DÍN YILDIZ.

AR

SILVER.*

20 — Ghazní [60]3 or 6

Obv. Area, within double square, similar to 6.

Margin, in segments outside,

ضرب هذا | . . . . | غزنة فى . . . | . . ـب و . . . . . .

Rev. Area, within double square, similar to 6.

Margin, in segments outside, ... | . . . . |

عبده ومولاه | تاج الد ن[يا

AR 1·2, Wt. 103

21 — Ghazní? 610

Obv. Area, as 6.

Margin, in segments,

. . . . | همر . . . . | شهو . . . . | عشر وستمائة

Rev. Area, within double square,

السلطان
المعز

Margin, in segments,

عبده ومولاه تاج | الدنيا والد | ين يلدز | السلطانى

Pl. I. (Th. 23.) AR 1·15, Wt. 101

---

* Cf. nos. 7 and 8.

COPPER.

Æ No.	Mint: Date	Obv.	Rev.	
22, 23		Bull Nandí to left, standing. Above, debased Hindí characters.	معز الدنيا والدين عبده يلدز over ين, star.	Æ ·6 Pl. I. Æ ·55
24—26		Chohán Horseman to right.* Beneath horse, a star. Traces of श्री हमीर: much debased.	السلطان المعظم ابو الفتح يلدز السلطانى	Pl. I. (Th. 24.) Æ ·65 Æ ·6 Æ ·6
27, 28		السلطان الاعظم معز[ز الدنيا والد ين	عبده الم]لك المعز تا]ج الدنيا و الدين يلدز	Æ ·65 Æ
29		. . . . . تاج الدنيا و [ال]دين يلدز	. . . . الملك . . . . . تاج الدن	Æ ·6

* The Chohán Horseman is always to right, the Bull Nandí to left.

KANAUJ ISSUE.

GOLD.

AV No.	Mint: Date.	*Obv.*	*Rev.*
30	[Kanauj]	The Goddess Lakshmí seated facing.	श्री म[ह *Ṣrí Maha-* मद वेने *mad vene* साम *Sám.* AV ·85, Wt. 66
31	[Kanauj]	Similar.	श्री महम *Ṣrí Mahama-* द साम *d Sám.* Pl. I. AV ·6, Wt. 65
32, 33	[Kanauj]	Similar.	श्री ह *Ṣrí Ha-* मीर मह[म *míraMahama-* द] साम *d Sám* AV ·6, Wt. 65 AV ·6, Wt. 66

III.—ÁRÁM SHÁH.

A.H. 607.

COPPER.

No.		*Obv.*	*Rev.*
34		Chohán Horseman, degraded.	ابو] المظفر ا]رامشا[ه ال]سلطا[ن Pl. II. Æ ·6

IV.—SHAMS-AD-DÍN ALTAMSH.

A.H. 607—633.

Æ

No. | Mint : Date. | SILVER.

35 Obv., within double square enclosed in circle,

لا اله الا الله
محمد رسول الله

In each segment, three dots.

Rev. (as obv.) في عهد الامام
المستنصر امير
المومنين

In each segment, three dots.

The first ا of الامام written very small and joined to the ل.

Traces of marginal inscription outside circle.

(Th. xxviii.) Æ 1·1, Wt. 163

36 6xx Obv. Area, within circle,

لا اله الا الله
محمد رسول الله
المستنصر بالله
امير المومنين

(The lám of the اله and alif of الله connected by an arch.)

Margin, ستمائة .... ضرب هذا ا

Rev. Area, within double square,

السلطان الاعظم
شمس الدنيا والدين
ابو المظفر التتم[ش
ا]لسلطا[ن] ناصر ا[مير المومنين

Margin, in segments, illegible (or ornaments, Th.).

Pl. II. (Th. xxx.) Æ 1·15, Wt. 164

AR No.	Mint: Date.	
37	63*x*	Obv. Area, within double square, enclosed in circle, فی عهد الامام المستنصر امیر المومنین In each segment, three dots. Margin, ... ضرب هذا الفضة Rev. Area as 36, but omitting ناصر امیر المومنین In each segments, three dots. Margin, ثلثین وستمائة .... ضرب PL. II. (Th. 31.) AR 1·15, Wt. 169

COPPER.

Æ No.	Mint: Date.	Obv.	Rev.
38—42	[Dehlí Th.]	Chohán Horseman. Around, सी हमीरः *Srí Hamírah*	Bull Nandí. Around, सुरितण सी समसदीण *Suritan Srí Samasadín* 38, *Jhul* ५, side ।। Pl. II. Æ ·6 39, „ F „ ।। Æ ·55 40, 41, „ ? „ ४ (Th. 42.) Æ ·6 Æ ·65 42, „ ∩ „ ।ℸ Æ ·6

BASE SILVER.

(Struck by Chohár Deva of Narwar.)

AR No.	Mint: Date.	Obv.	Rev.
43—45	[Narwar.]	Chohán Horseman. Around, श्री चाहड देव *Srí Cháhada Deva*	Bull Nandí. Around, असावरी श्री समसोरल देव *Asávari Srí Samasorala Deva* *Jhul* ш, side । Pl. II. (Th. 40.) AR ·65, Wt. 52 AR ·6, Wt. 51 I. O. C. AR ·6, Wt. 52

COPPER.

Æ No.	Mint: Date.	Obv.	Rev.
46, 47	[Rantambhor? Th.] Samvat 1283 A.H. [62]3	श्र]ी सुलता *Srí Sultá(na)* लितितिमि *Lititimi* सि सं १२[८३ *si Sam* 1283 Date, 46, 12.. 47, 1283	Within circle, السلطان ایلتتمش Around 46, ... ضرب „ 47, سنة ثلث............ .... (Th. 44.) Æ ·6 Pl. II. Æ ·65

Æ No.	Mint: Date.	*Obv.*	*Rev.*
48—50		Chohán Horseman. Around, सी *Srí*	شمس الدنيا والدين ايـ]ـلـتـتـمـش السلطان Pl. II. (Th. 48.) Æ ·6 Æ ·6 Æ ·6
51, 52		,, सी ह *Srí Ha(míraḥ)*	شمس الدنيا والدين ابو المظ[فر ايلـتـتمش السلط[ان Pl. II. Æ ·55 Æ ·6
53	Multán.	Within square, enclosed in circle, عدل السلطـــان	Within hexagram, enclosed in circle, ضـــرب ملـتـان Pl. II. (Th. 49.) Æ ·65
54	Dehlí.	Within octagram, enclosed in circle, Same.	Within octagram, enclosed in circle, ·حضرت دهـلـى (Th. 53.) Æ ·55
55	Dehlí.	Within circle, عدل السلـــطـان المعـظـ[م]	Within circle, ضرب بحضرت دهـــلـى Æ ·55

Æ No.	Mint: Date.	Obv.	Rev.
56, 57		Within hexagram, عدل	Within hexagram, السلطان (Th. 52.) Æ ·55 Æ ·55
58		Within circle, عدل	Within circle, شمس Above, ornament. (Th. 55.) Æ ·5
59		Within zigzag border, Traces of Hindí inscription.	Within zigzag border, Same. (Th. 54.) Æ ·5
60		Within hexagram, سلطان	Within hexagram, التتمش Æ ·55

V.—RUKN-AD-DÍN FÍRÓZ SHÁH I.

A.H. 633—634.

COPPER.

Æ No.	Mint: Date.	Obv.	Rev.
61		Chohán Horseman; traces of usual Hindí inscription (ह).	Bull Nandí: on *Jhul* ل, on side ।।। Above, ... रुकण दीण *Rukaṇa díṇ* Pl. II. (Th. 89.) Æ ·6

VI.—RIZÍYAH.

A.H. 634—637.

SILVER.

AR No.	Mint: Date.	
62	Lakhnautí (Gaur).	Obv. Area, within double-square enclosed in circle, فی عهد الامام المستنصر امیر المومـــنیـــن In each segment, dot. Margin, ... الفضة بلكنوتی سنة ..... Rev. السلطان الاعظم جلالـــة الدنـيا والـديـن ملكة ابنت اليتمش السلطـان نصرة امیر المومنین PL. II. (Th. 90.) AR 1·1, Wt. 165

COPPER.

Æ	Obv.	Rev.
63, 64	Chohán Horseman, and *Srí Hamírah*	السلطان .... رضية ..... الدنـيا والـديـن

PL. II. (Th. 91.) Æ ·6
Æ ·65

Æ

No.	Mint: Date.	Obv.	Rev.
65, 66		Chohán Horseman, and *Srí Hamírah*	السلطان المعظم رضـ[ية الدين بنت؟ السلطان Æ ·55 PL. II. Æ ·55

VII.—MU'IZZ-AD-DÍN BAHRÁM-SHÁH.

A.H. 637—639.

SILVER.

AR

67 [Dehlí] Obv. Area, within double square enclosed in circle,

فى عهد الامام
المستنصر امير
المومنين

In each segment, three dots.

Margin, ... ضرب هذا السكة بحضرت

Rev. Area (as obv.), السلطن الاعظم
معز الدنيا والدين
ابو المظفر بهرامشاه
بن السلطان

In segments, ناصر | امير | المو | منين

Margin, ضرب .... سنة ثمان وثلثين وستمائة

PL. II. (Th.92.) AR 1·15, Wt. 167

COPPER.

Æ No.	Mint: Date.	*Obv.*	*Rev.*
68		Chohán Horseman. Above, بن سلطان	Within square, enclosed in circle, السلــطـ[ـان الاعظم معـ[ـز الدنيا والد]ين In segments, loops. Pl. II. (Th. 93.) Æ ·6
69		Chohán Horseman. Illegible inscription.	Same. Pl. II. Æ ·6
70—72		Chohán Horseman. Around, स्री हमीर: *Srí Hamírah̥*	Bull Nandí. Around, सुरिताण स्रीमुअजदीं *Suritáṇ Srí Muajadíṃ* on *Jhul* +, on side ε (Th. 94.) Æ ·6 Pl. II. Æ ·6 Æ ·55

VIII. — 'ALÁ-AD-DÍN MAS'ÚD SHÁH.

A.H. 639—644.

Æ No.	Mint: Date.	SILVER.
73	Dehlí [639-40*]	Obv. Area, within double square enclosed in circle, فی عهد الامام المستنصر امیر المومنین In segments . . . Margin (traces of) ..... بحضرت دهلی .... Rev. Area (as obv.), السلطان الاعظم علا الدنیا والدین ابو المظفر مسعود شاه بن السلطان In segments, . . . Margin obliterated. Pl. III. (Th. 97.) Æ 1·0, Wt. 168

* The Khalífah Al-Mustansir died in A.H. 640.

Æ No.	Mint: Date.	
74	641	Same as 73: but on obv. area المستعصم instead of المستنصر Obv. and rev. margins, ضرب . . . . سنة احد واربعين وستمائة (Th. 98.) Æ 1·05. Wt. 169
75	[6]42	Same as 74: but obv. margin .... اثنين اربعين وس ..... Rev. margin obliterated. Æ 1·05, Wt. 167
76, 77		Similar to 74. Mint and date obliterated. Æ 1·05, Wt. 163 Æ 1·05, Wt. 168

COPPER.

Æ No.	Mint: Date.	Obv.	Rev.
78—80		Chohán Horseman. Above, مسعود شاه	السلـطـــان الاعـظـم عـلا الدنيا والدين (Th. 99.) Æ ·65 Æ ·6 Æ ·65
81		Same.	… … الاعـظـم عـلا الدنيا والدين مـسـعـود شـاه (Blundered.) Pl. III. (Th. 102.) Æ ·6
82		Chohán Horseman. Above, श्री . . . . *Srí*	[ال]سلـطـــان . . . عظم عـلا الدنيا والدين … ….. (The connecting stroke before ـعظم seems to point to the form المعظم.) Pl. III. Æ ·6
83		Horseman, very rude.	. . . . الا . . . . مـــســعـــود بن سل[طان] (Th. 103.) Æ ·65
84		Chohán Horseman.	Bull Nandí. Above, श्र]लादिण *A*]*ládiṇ*. (Th. 105.) Æ ·6

IX. — NÁṢIR-AD-DÍN MAHMÚD SHÁH I.

A.H. 644—664.

Æ No.	Mint: Date.	SILVER.
85		Obv. Area, within double square enclosed in circle, فـــى عـهـد الامـام المستنصر باالله امير الـمـومـنـيـن لـلـه Rev. Area (as obv.), السلـطـان الاعـــظـــم ناصـر الـدنـيـا والـديـن ابـو الـمـظـفـر مـحـمـود شـاه بـــن سلـــطـــان Apparently no margins. PL. III. (Th. 60.*) Æ 1·1, Wt. 161

* See the *Chronicles of the Pathan kings of Dehli* for Mr. Thomas's reasons for ascribing this coin to an elder brother of Maḥmood, who died in 626. I am rather inclined to believe that the occurrence of Al-Mustansir's name is merely another instance of the use of an old obverse, of which many examples could be quoted. See *Introduction*.

Æ No.	Mint: Date.	
86	Dehlí 654	Obv. Area (as 85), فى عهد الامام المستعصم امير المومنين In top and bottom segments, an annulet. Margin, ضرب هذه الفضة بحضرت دهلى فى سنة اربع خمسين وستمائة Rev. Area same as 85; but omitting شاه, and substituting ابن for بن. In top and bottom segments, annulet; in right and left, ... Margin as obv. margin, but partly obliterated. (Th. 106.) Æ 1·05, Wt. 165
87	Dehlí 655	Same as 86: but date خمس خمسين وستمائة on both margins. Pl. III. (Th. 106.) Æ 1·1, Wt. 166
88, 89	Dehlí 657	Same: but date سبع خمسين وستمائة (Th. 106.) Æ 1·05, Wt. 166 Æ 1·05, Wt. 168
90	Dehlí 658	Same: but date ثمان خمسين وسبمائة (Th. 106.) Æ 1·05, Wt. 170
91	Dehlí 660	Same: but date ستين وستمائة (Th. 106.) Æ 1·0, Wt 169

AR No.	Mint: Date.	
92	Dehlí 662	Same : but date اثنين وستين وستمائة (ابن vice بن) (Th. 106.) AR 1·05, Wt. 167
93	Dehlí 664	Same : but date اربع وستين وستمائة (ابن vice بن) (Th. 106.) AR 1·05, Wt. 167
94, 95		Similar : Mint and date obliterated. AR 1·15, Wt. 167; AR 1·1, Wt. 169

COPPER.

Æ	Obv.	Rev.
96—98	Chohán Horseman : Above, محمو[د] In front, श्री हमी[र: *Ṣrí Hamí[raḥ]*	السلطان الا عظم ناصر الد نيا والدين (Th. 107.) Æ ·6 PL. III. Æ ·6 Æ ·6
99	Same.	Same, but arranged ا]لسلطان الاعظم ناصر الدنيا والدين PL. III. Æ ·6

No.	Mint: Date.	

X.—GHIYÁS-AD-DÍN BALBAN.

A.H. 664—686.

GOLD.

AV

100 | Dehlí 672 | Obv. Area, within circle,

الامام
المستعصم امير
المومنين

Margin, ضرب هذه السكة بحضرت دهلی فی سنة اثنين وسبعين وستمائة

Rev. Area, within circle,

السلطان الاعظم
غياث الدنيا والدين
ابو المظفر بلبن
السلطان

Margin same as obv., partly obliterated.

PL. III. (Cf. Th. 111.) AV 1·15, Wt. 169

101 | Dehlí 675 | Same: but date خمس وسبعين وستمائة

Rev. margin nearly illegible.

AV 1·1, Wt. 168

102 | Dehlí 678 | Same: but date ثمان وسبعين وستمائة on both margins.

AV 1·05, Wt. 169

Æ No.	Mint : Date.	
		SILVER.
103, 104	Dehlí 664	Obv. Area, within double square, enclosed in circle, الامام المستعصم امير المومنين Annulet in top and bottom segments. Margin, ضرب هذه الفضة بحضرت دهلى فى سنة اربع وستين وستمائة Rev. Area (as obv.), السلطان الاعظم غياث الدنيا والدين ابو المظفر بلبن السلطان In segments above and beneath, annulet ; at right and left, . . Margin, traces similar to obv. PL. III. (Th. 112.) Æ 1·1, Wt. 165 Æ 1·1, Wt. 164
105	Dehlí 664	Similar : but السكة *vice* الفضة, and no . . at sides. (Badly engraved, and blundered.) Æ 1·15, Wt. 167
106	Dehlí 665	Same as 103 : but date خمس وستين وستمائة on both margins. (Th. 112.) Æ 1·15, Wt. 169

Æ No.	Mint: Date.	
107	Dehlí 667	Same: without . . ; date سبع وستين وستمائة on obv. margin. Rev. margin obliterated. (Th. 112.) Æ 1·1, Wt. 167
108, 109	Dehlí 669	Same as 103: date تسعة وستين وس[تمائة] on both margins. (Th. 112.) Æ 1·1, Wt. 167 Æ 1·15, Wt. 166
110	Dehlí 673	Same: without . . ; date ثلاث وسبعين وستمائة on both margins. (Th. 112.) Æ 1·15, Wt. 168
111	Dehlí 674	Same: without . . ; date اربع وسبعين وستمائة on obv. margin. Rev. margin obliterated. (Th. 112.) Æ 1·15, Wt. 165
112–114	Dehlí	Similar to 103: dates illegible. Æ 1·1, Wt. 165 Æ 1·1, Wt. 169 Æ 1·1, Wt 167

COPPER.

Æ No.	Mint : Date	Obv.	Rev.	
115-118		In centre, within circle, بلبن Around, श्रीः सुलतां गयासुदीं *Ṣríḥ Sultáṃ Gyásudíṃ.*	Within double square, السلطان الا عظم غياث الد نيا والدين	PL. III. (Th. 113.) Æ ·65 Æ ·65 Æ ·65 Æ ·65
119, 120		السلطان الاعظم	غياث الدنيا والدين	PL. III. (Th. 114.) Æ ·65 Æ ·5
121, 122	Dehlí	عدل غياثی	بحضرت دهلی	(Th. 115.) Æ ·5 PL. III. Æ ·55

XI.—MU'IZZ-AD-DÍN KAI-KUBÁD.

A.H. 686—689.

AV No.	Mint: Date.	GOLD.
123	Dehlí 687	Obv. Area, within circle, الامام المستعصم امير المومنين Margin, ضرب هذه السكة بحضرت د[هلی فی سنة] سبع وثمانين وستماىة Rev. Area, within circle, السلطان الاعظم معز الدنيا والدين ابو المظفر كيقباد السلطان Margin, traces, as obv. PL. III. AV 1·1, Wt. 169

Æ No.	Mint: Date.	SILVER.
124, 125	Dehlí 686	Same: but areas enclosed in double square within circle, and obv. margin ضرب هذه ال....... دهلى فى سنة ست وثمانين وستماىة Rev. margin obliterated. Æ 1·2, Wt. 167 Æ 1·25, Wt. 166
126	Dehlí 687	Same: date سبع وثمانين وستماىة on both margins, but traces on rev. only. (Th. 116.) Æ 1·2, Wt. 168
127	Dehlí 688	Same: date ثمان وثمانين وستماىة on obv. margin. Rev. margin obliterated. (Th. 116.) Æ 1·2, Wt. 162
128	Dehlí	Similar, but الفضة : date obliterated on both sides. Æ 1·2, Wt. 165

COPPER.

Æ No.	Mint: Date.	Obv.	Rev.
129, 130		كيقباد स्री सुलता[ं] मुइजुद[ीं] *Srí Sultám* *Muijudim.*	Within border, السلطان الا عظم معز الد نيا والدين Pl. III. (Th. 117.) Æ ·75 Æ ·65
131-133		السلطان الاعظم	معز الدنيا والدين Pl. III. (Th. 118.) Æ ·7 Æ ·65 Æ ·65
134, 135		Within ornamented borders, معز الدنيا	والد ين Æ ·6 Pl. III. Æ ·65
136	Dehlí	عدل معزى	بحضرت دهلى (Th. 9.) Æ ·55
137		عدل	معز[ى] Æ ·5

SECOND DYNASTY.

XII.—JALÁL-AD-DÍN FÍROZ II.

A.H. 689—695.

AV No.	Mint: Date.	GOLD.
138	Dehlí 695	Obv. Area, within circle, الامام المستعصم امير المومنين Margin, ضرب هذه السكة بحضرة دهلى فى سنة خمس وتسعين وستمائة Rev. [الـ]سلطان الاعظم [جـ]لال الدنيا والدين ابو المظفر فيروز شاه [ا]لسلطان PL. IV. (Th. 120.) AV 1·0, Wt. 166

Æ No.	Mint: Date.	SILVER.
139	[Dehlí] 68[9]	Obv. Area, within double square enclosed in circle (annulets in top and bottom segments), الامام المستعصم امير المومنين Margin, وثمانين وستمائة .... Rev. Area as 138, but within double square: margin obliterated. (Th. 121.) Æ 1·15, Wt. 167
140, 141	Dehlí 690	Same: but ضرب هذه ال[فضة] بحضرت دهلى فى سنة تسعين وستمائة on obv. margin; rev. margin obliterated. (Th. 121.) Æ 1·15, Wt. 165 (Ringed.) Æ 1·15
142	Dehlí 691	Same: but date احدى وتسعين وستمائة on obv. margin; traces on rev. margin. Pl. IV. (Th. 121.) Æ 1·15, Wt. 163
143	Dehlí 693	Same: but امير in last line of obv. (as 138): and date ثلث وتسعين وستمائة on obv. margin. Rev. margin obliterated, and حضرة with ة.* (Th. 121.) Æ 1·15, Wt. 169

* Generally so spelt henceforward.

Æ No.	Mint : Date.		
144	Dehlí 694	Same as 143 : but date اربع وتسعين وستمائة on obv. margin. Rev. margin obliterated. (Th. 121.) Æ 1·2, Wt. 169	
145	Dehlí 695	Same : but date خمس وتسعين وستمائة on obv. margin. Rev. margin obliterated. (Th. 121.) Æ 1·1, Wt. 169	

COPPER.

Æ		*Obv.*	*Rev.*
146–148		In centre, شـــاه فـيـروز Around, श्रीः सुलतां जलालुदीं *Ṣríḥ Sultáṃ Jaláludíṃ*	السلـطـــان الا عظم جلال الد نيـا والـديـــن Pl. IV. (Th. 122.) Æ ·65 Æ ·7 Æ ·7
149–151		السلطان الاعـظـم	جـلال الـد نـيا والـديـن (Th. 123.) Æ ·65 Pl. IV. Æ ·65 Æ ·75
152, 152*a*	Dehlí	Within octagram, عدل فيروز شاه	Within octagram, بحضرت دهـلـى (Th. 124.) Æ ·6 Æ ·6

XIII.—RUKN-AD-DÍN IBRÁHÍM SHÁH I.

A.H. 695.

Æ No.	Mint: Date.	SILVER.
153	Dehlí 695	Obv. Area, within double square, السلطان الاعظم ركن الدنيا والدين ابو المظفر ابراهيم شاه السلطان بن Margin obliterated. Rev. Area, within circle, السلطان الاعظم جلال الدنيا والدين فيروز شاه ناصر امير المومنين Margin, ضرب هذه الفضة بحضرة دهلى فى سنة خمس وتسعين وستمائة PL. IV. (Th. 126.) Æ 1·25, Wt. 166

COPPER.

Æ No.	Mint: Date.	Obv.	Rev.
154, 155		السلطان الا عظم ركن الد نيا والدين	ابراهيم شاه بن فيروز شاه Pl. IV. (Th. 127.) Æ ·7 Æ ·6
156		عدل ابراهيم شاه	بن فيروز شاه (Th. 129.) Æ ·6

XIV.—'ALÁ-AD-DÍN MUHAMMAD SHÁH I.

A.H. 695—715.

GOLD.

AV No.	Mint: Date.	
157	Dehlí 698	Obv. السلطان الاعظم علا الدنيا والدين ابو المظفر محمد شاه السلطان Rev. Area, within circle, سكندر الثانى يمين الخلافة ناصر امير المومنين Margin, ضرب هذه السكة بحضرة د[هلى فى سنة] ثمان تسعين وستمائة Pl. IV. AV 1·05, Wt. 170

AV No.	Mint: Date.	
158	Dehlí 704	Same : date اربع وسبعمائة (Th. 130.) AV 1·0, Wt. 170
159	*Dár-al-Islám.* [Dehlí] 708	Same : but margin ضرب هذه السكة بدار الاسلام فى سنة ثمان وسبعمائة AV 1·0, Wt. 169
160	Dehlí 710	Same : but بحضرة دهلى فى سنة عشر وسبعمائة AV 1·05, Wt. 167
161	715	Same : date سنة خمس عشر وسبعمائة AV ·95, Wt. 164
162, 163		Same area inscriptions, but both enclosed in double squares within circles ; annulet in each segment. Margins obliterated. AV ·9, Wt. 169 (Th. 131.) AV ·85, Wt. 165

SILVER.

AR		
164, 165	Dehlí 695	Same area inscriptions, both enclosed in double squares within circles ; annulet in each segment. Rev. margin, ضرب هذه الفضة بحضرة دهلى فى سنة خمس وتسعين وستمائة Pl. IV. (Th. 132.) AR 1·1, Wt. 169 AR 1·1, Wt. 171

Æ No.	Mint: Date.	
166	697*	Same : but ..نة سبع وتسعين وستماية Æ 1·15, Wt. 169
167	699	Same : but .... فى سنة تسع وتسعين ... (Th. 132.) Æ 1·1, Wt. 166
168	703	Same : but .....نة ثلاث وسبعماية (Th. 132.) Æ 1·0, Wt. 169
169	Dehlí 705	Same : but ...... دهلى فى سنة خمس وسبعماية (Th. 132.) Æ 1·0, Wt. 171
170, 171	710	Same : but ..... سنة عشر وسبعماية (Th. 132.) Æ 1·0, Wt. 166 Æ 1·0, Wt. 166
172	Dehlí 711	Same : but ......ة دهلى فى سنة احدى عشر وسبعماية (Th. 132.) Æ 1·05, Wt. 167
173	*Dár-al-Islám.* (Dehlí) 711	Same : but بدار الاسلام فى سنة احدى عشر وسبعماية Æ 1·0, Wt. 170
174	Dehlí 712	Same : but بحضرة دهلى فى سنة اثنى عشر وسبعماية (Th. 132.) Æ 1·1, Wt. 170
175, 176	Dehlí 713	Same : but ثلاث عشر وسبعماية (Th. 132.) Æ 1·05, Wt. 163 Æ 1·05, Wt. 167

* Although the name of the mint is obliterated, we are safe in ascribing these coins (nos. 166—168, 170, 171) to Dehlí.

Æ No.	Mint: Date.	
177	*Dár-al-Islám* (Dehlí) [7]13	Same: but .... بدار الاسلام فی سنة ثلاث عشر (Th. 133.) Æ 1·0, Wt. 170
178, 179	Dehlí 714	Same: but بحضرة دهلی فی سنة اربع عشر وسبعمائة (Th. 132.) Æ 1·05, Wt. 170 Æ 1·05, Wt. 167
180	Dehlí 715	Same: but خمس (Th. 132.) Æ 1·05, Wt. 170
181	Dehlí *xx*6	Same: but date ....ست و ? Æ 1·15, Wt. 163

Æ

COPPER.

A.

		Obv.	*Rev.*
182	700	In centre, within circle, محمد شاه Around, श्रीः सुल्तां अलावदीं ७०० *Ṣríḥ Sultáṃ Alávadíṃ*, 700	السلطان [الا عظم علا ا[لد نيـ]ـا والـ[ـدين (Th. 136.) Æ ·65
183–185	701	,, but ७०१	,, (Th. 136.) Æ ·6 Æ ·6 Æ ·6
186	702	,, ७०२	,, (Th. 136.) Æ ·6
187	704	,, ७०४	,, (Th. 136.) Æ ·6

Æ No.	Mint: Date.		
188	705	Same as 182; but ٧٠٥	Same as 182. (Th. 136.) Æ ·6
189	706 ?	„ ٧٠٦	„ Æ ·7
190	710	„ ٧١٠	„ Pl. IV. (Th. 136.) Æ ·65
191	711	„ ٧١١	„ (Th. 136.) Æ ·7
192–194		Same: years obscure.	Æ ·6 Æ ·7 Æ ·7

B.

Æ No.	Mint: Date.		
195	701	السلطان [الا عظم علا الد نيا والدين	ابو المظفر محمد شاه السلطان ١ ٧ (*sic*) Pl. IV. Æ ·65
196	702	„	„ ٧٢ ٠ (Th. 135.) Æ ·6
197	703	„	„ ٧٣ ٠ (Th. 135.) Æ ·6
198	712	„	„ ٧١٢ (Th. 135.) Æ ·65

Æ No.	Mint : Date.	Obverse	Reverse
199	713	Same as 195.	Same as 195; but ٧١٣ (Th. 135.) Æ ·65
200	714	„	„ ٧١۴ (Th. 135.) Æ ·65
201	715	„	„ ٧١۵ (Th. 135.) Æ ·65

C.

Æ No.	Mint : Date.	Obverse	Reverse
202, 203		السلطان الاعظم	علا الد نيا والدين (Th. 137.) Æ ·65 Æ ·65
204	Dehlí	عدل محمد شاه	بحضرة دهلى (Th. 138.) Æ ·5

XV.—SHIHÁB-AD-DÍN 'UMAR SHÁH.

A.H. 715.

COPPER

Æ No.	Mint : Date.	Obverse	Reverse
205	715	السلطان الا عظم شهاب ال[د نيـ]ـا والدين	ابو المظفر عمر شاه السلطان ٧١۵ Pl. IV. (Th 141.) Æ ·6

No.	Mint: Date.	

XVI.—ḲUṬB-AD-DÍN MUBÁRAK SHÁH I.

A.H. 716—720.

SQUARE.

GOLD.

AV

206 *Dár-al-Khiláfah.* (Dehlí) 718

Obv.

الامـــام الاعـظـم
خليفة رب العالمين
قطب الدنيا والدين
ابو المظفر مباركشاه

Rev. Area, within square,

السلـطـــان ابـن
السلـطـان الواثـــق
بالله امير المومنين

Margin, ضرب هذه السكة | بحضرة دارالخلافة | فى سنة ثمان | عشر وسبعمائة |

PL. IV. (Th. 142.) AV ·9, Wt. 167

207 *Dár-al-Khiláfah.* (Dehlí) 719

Same: but تسع

(Th. 142.) AV 1·0, Wt. 169

SILVER.

AR

208 *Dár-al-Khiláfah.* (Dehlí) 718

Same as 206.

AR ·95, Wt. 168

No.	Mint: Date.	

ROUND.

Æ

SILVER.

209, 210 — Dehlí 716

Obv.

السلطان الاعظم
قطب الدنيا والدين
ابو المظفر مباركشاه
السلطان بن السلطان

Rev. Area, within circle,

اسكندر الزمان
يمين الخلافة ناصر
امير المومنين

Margin, ضرب هذه الفضة بحضرة دهلى فى سنة ست عشر وسبعمائة .

PL. IV. (Th. 143). Æ 1·05, Wt. 169
Æ 1·05, Wt. 169

211 — Dehlí 717

Same: but سبع

(Th. 143.) Æ 1·05, Wt. 170

212, 213 — *Dár-al-Mulk.* (Dehlí) 717

Obv.

الامام الاعظم
قطب الدنيا والدين
ابو المظفر خليفة الله

Rev. Area, within circle,

مباركشاه السلطان
ابن السلطان الواثق
بالله امير المومنين

Margin, ضرب هذه الفضة بحضرة دار الملك فى سنة سبع عشر وسبعمائة

(Th. 146.) Æ 1·05, Wt. 168
Æ 1·1, Wt. 169

COPPER.

Æ

A.

No.	Mint: Date.	Obv.	Rev.	
214	716	السلطان الا عظم قطب الد نيا والدين	ابو المظفر مبارك شاه السلطان ٧]١٦	(Th. 147.) Æ ·55

B.

No.	Mint: Date.	Obv.	Rev.	
215	716	,,	مباركشاه السلطان بن السلطان ٧١٦	Pl. IV. (Th. 148.) Æ ·7
216	717	,,	٧١٧ ,,	(Th. 148.) Æ ·65

C.

No.	Mint: Date.	Obv.	Rev.	
217, 218	717	الامام الاعظم قطب الدنيا والدين ٧١٧	ابو المظفر مباركشاه السلطان ابن] السل[طان	(Th. 149.) Æ ·65 Æ ·65
219, 220	719	٧١٩ ,,	,,	(Th. 149.) Æ ·65 Æ ·7

Æ No.	Mint: Date.	Obv.	Rev.	
		D.		
221, 222	717	خليفة رب العالمين قطب الدنيا والدين ابو المظفر ٧١٧	مباركشاه السلطان ابن السلطان الواثق بالله امير المومنين	(Th. 150.) Æ ·7 Æ ·7
		E.		
223, 224		,, omitting last line and date.	مباركشاه ابو المظفر السلطان ابن السلطان الواثق بالله	Æ ·7 Æ ·7

SQUARE.

Æ No.	Mint: Date.	Obv.	Rev.	
		F.		
225, 226	718	Within square, قطب الدنيا والدين Outside, خليفة | الله | ابو ا | لمظفر	مباركشاه السلطان ابن السلطان ٧١٨	(Th. 151.) Æ ·6 Pl. IV. Æ ·6
227	719	,,	,, ٧١٩	(Th. 151.) Æ ·6
228	720	,,	,, ٧٢٠	(Th. 151.) Æ ·55

G.

Æ No.	Mint: Date.	*Obv.*	*Rev.*
229,	719	الامام الا عظم قطب الد نيا والدين	خليفة الله مباركشاه السلطان ابن السلطان ٧١٩ Æ ·6
230–232	720	,,	٧٢٠ ,, (Th. 152.) Æ ·6 Æ ·6 Æ ·7

H.

Æ No.	Mint: Date.	*Obv.*	*Rev.*
232*a*		الامـــام الاعظـــم	قطب الدنيا والـــديـــن (Th. 153.) Æ ·55
233, 234	*Dár-al-Khiláfah* (Dehlí)	عـــدل مباركشاه	بحضرت دار الخلافة (Th. 154.) Æ ·45 Æ ·45

No.	Mint: Date.	

XVII.—NÁSIR-AD-DÍN KHUSRÚ SHÁH.

A.H. 720.

GOLD.

AV

235 | Dehlí 720 | Obv., within double square,

السلطان الاعظم
ناصر الدنيا والدين
ابو المظفر

Rev. Area, within circle,

خسرو شاه السلطان
الواثق بنصر الرحمن
ولی امیر المومنین

Margin ضرب هذه السكة بحضرة دهلى فى سنة عشرين وسبعمائة

PL. IV. (*Cf.* Th. 155.) AV ·95, Wt. 161

COPPER.

Æ

236 | 720 |

السلطان الا
عظم ناصر الدنيا
والدين ۷۲۰

In centre, within circle,

شاه
خسرو

Around,

السلطان ولی امیر المومنین

PL. IV. (Th. 156.) Æ ·6

No.	Mint: Date.	AV

THIRD DYNASTY.

XVIII.—GHÍYAS-AD-DÍN TAGHLAK SHÁH I.

A.H. 720—725.

GOLD.

237 Obv. Area, within double square,

السلـــطـان الغازی

غیاث الدنیا وا[لدین

ابو الـــمـــظـــفـر

Rev. Area, an old obv. area of Muhammad's, same as 161.

Margin illegible.

(Th. 157.) AV 1·0, Wt. 173

238 Dehlí 720 Obv. Area, within double square,

السلـــطـان الغازی

غیاث الدنیا والدین

ابو المـــظـــفـــر

Rev. Area, within circle,

تغلق شاه

السلـــطـــان نـاصر

امیر المومنین

Margin, ضرب هذه السکة بحضر[ة] دهلی فی سنة عشرین وسبعمائة

AV 1·0, Wt. 169

AV No.	Mint: Date.	
239	Dehlí 722	Same : but اثنى وعشرين وسبعمائة AV ·95, Wt. 170
240	Dehlí 724	Same : but اربع (Th. 159.) AV ·95, Wt. 168
241	Dehlí 726 *Posthumous.*	Obv. Area السلطان السعيد الشهيد الغازى غياث الدنيا والدين Rev. Area, within circle, ابو المظفر تغلقشاه السلطان (؟)* انار الله برهانه Margin, ضرب هذه السكة فى حضر[ة] د... سنة ست وعشرين وسبعمائة Pl. V. (Th. 158.) AV ·9, Wt. 170
242		Obv. Area, غياث الدنيا والدين ناصر امير المومنين Rev. Area, within circle, المتوكل على الله ابو المظفر تغلق شاه Margin illegible. AV ·95, Wt. 164

* Mr. Thomas has read the letters following تغلقشاه as a date, ٧٢١. Apart from the improbability of a date in ciphers upon a gold coin of this period, and the fact that a different date (726) occurs in the marginal inscription, the letters themselves do not favour the supposition. The supposed ٧ is لط, and I believe the whole word is a badly written السلطان.

SILVER.

Æ No.	Mint: Date.	
243	Deógír 721	Areas as 238. Obv. margin, ضرب هذه السكة بقلعة ديوگير فی سنة احدی عشرين وسبعمائة Pl. V. (Th. 160.) Æ 1·15, Wt. 170
244	721	Same: but mint (between السكة and سنة) obliterated and و inserted. Æ 1·1, Wt. 169
245	Dehlí 722	Same: but بحضرة دهلی فی سنة اثنی وعشرين وسبعمائة (Th. 161.) Æ 1·05, Wt. 169
246	Dehlí 723	Same: but ثلاث (Th. 161.) Æ 1·1, Wt. 170
247	Dehlí 724	Same: but اربع (Th. 161.) Æ 1·1, Wt. 169
248	Dehlí 725	Same: but خمس Æ 1·05, Wt. 168
248*a*		Similar to 241: margins cut off. Æ ·6

COPPER.

A

Æ No.	Mint: Date.	Obv.	Rev.
249, 250	721	السلطان الغازى غياث الـــدنيا والدين	ابو الـــمظـفر تـغـلـــق شاه السلطان ۷۲۱ (Th. 164.) Æ ·6 Æ ·65
251	722	"	" ۷۲۲ Pl. V. (Th. 164.) Æ ·65
252	723	"	" ۷]۲۳ (Th. 164.) Æ ·65
253	724	"	" ۷]۲۴ (Th. 164.) Æ ·6
254	725	"	" ۷]۲۵ (Th. 164.) Æ ·6

Æ No.	Mint: Date.	Obv.	Rev.
		B.	
255	721	Same as 249 : but at foot ٧٢١	In centre, شاه تغلق Around, श्रीः सुलतां गयासुदीं *Ṣríḥ Sultáṃ Gyásudíṃ* (Th. 163.) Æ ·6
256	725	,, ٧٢٥	,, Pl. V. Æ ·6
		C.	
257		السلطان الا غظم غياث الدنيا والدين	In centre, شاه تغلق Around, Arabic inscr. obliterated. Æ ·65
		D.	
258, 259		تغلق	شاه (Th. 165.) Æ ·55

AV No.	Mint: Date.	

XIX.—MUHAMMAD II. IBN TAGHLAḲ.

A.H. 725—752.

A.*

GOLD.

260-262 | Dehlí 726 | Obv.

اشـــهـــد ان لا
الـــه الا الـــلـــه
واسهـد ان محمـدا
عـــبده ورسـولـــه

Rev. Area, within circle,

الواثـــق بتـــائيد
الرحمن محـمـــد
شاه السلـــطـــان

Margin, ضرب هذا الدينار بحضرة دهلى سنة ست وعشرين وسبعمائة

PL. V. (Th. 171.) AV ·95, Wt. 199
AV ·95, Wt. 197
AV ·95, Wt. 198

SILVER.

AR

263 | Dehlí 725 | Same: but العدلى instead of الدينار; and خمس

(Th. 180.) AR 1·0, Wt. 151

* See no. 241, a posthumous coin of preceding Sultán.

B.

AV No.	Mint: Date.	GOLD.
264	Dehlí 727	Obv. Area, within circle, لا الــــه الا الــلـه محمد رسول الــلــه Margin, هذا الدينار بحضرة دهلى فى سنة سبع وعشرين وسبعمائة Rev. Area, ضـــرب فـــى زمن العبد الراجى رحمة الله محمد بن تغلق PL. V. (Th. 173.) AV ·7, Wt. 197

C.

		GOLD.
265	729	Obv. Area, within hexagonal border, ضرب فى زمن الـــعبد الـــراجـــى رحمة الـــلـــه مـحـمد بن Rev. Area, السلطان السعـــيـــد الشهيد تغلق شاه سنة تسع وعشرين وسبـعـمائة (Cf. Th. 179.) AV ·75, Wt. 168

No.	Mint: Date.	
AV		
266, 267	733	Sae as 265 : but date سنة ثلث ثلثين وسبعماية and بن in line with محمد AV ·75, Wt. 169 AV ·8, Wt. 169

SILVER.

No.	Mint: Date.	
AR		
268, 269	728	Same : but سنة ثمن وعشرين وسبعماية (Th. 182.) AR ·75, Wt. 139 AR ·75, Wt. 140
270	729	Same : but تسعة (Th. 182.) AR ·7, Wt. 140
271	729	Same : but تسع AR ·75, Wt. 140
272	730	Same : but ثلثين (Th. 182.) AR ·75, Wt. 137

COPPER.

No.	Mint: Date.	
Æ		
273		Same as 266: year uncertain. Æ ·75

Æ

No.	Mint: Date.	

D.

SILVER.

274 | Satgáon 730 | Obv. Area, within circle,

لا الــــه الا

الله محــمــد

رسول الــلــه

Margin, ضرب هذه السكة بستگانون فی سنة ثلثین وسبعمایة

Rev. Area,

ابو بكر

المجاهــد فــى

سبــيل الــلــه

محمد بن تغلق شاه

(Th. 184.) Æ ·95, Wt. 169

275 | Same: but obv. margin illegible, and محمد removed to middle line of rev.

Æ ·95, Wt. 169

AV No.	Mint: Date.	
		E.
		GOLD.
276, 277	Dehlí 736	Obv. Area, والله الغنى وانتم الفقرا٬ Rev. Area, within circle, فى عهد محمد بن تغلق Margin, بحضرة دهلى سنة ست وتلثين وسبعمائة (Th. 176.) AV ·7, Wt. 171 AV ·75, Wt. 168

SMALL COPPER.

F.

Æ		Obv.	Rev.
278, 279	725	المجاهد فى سبيل الله	محمد بن تغلقشاه ٧٢٥

(Th. 190.) Æ ·6
Æ ·6

Æ

G.

No.	Mint: Date.	*Obv.*	*Rev.*
280	726	السلطــــان الـــعـــادل	بن محـمـد ٧٢٦ تغلقشاه (Peculiar ligature in شاه) (Th. 189.) Æ ·6
281	727	"	" ٧٢٧ Pl. V. (Th. 189.) Æ ·55

H.

No.	Mint: Date.	*Obv.*	*Rev.*
282, 283	727	فی زمن السطان العادل محمد بن تـــغـــلـــقشاه	دامت سلطنته فی سنة سبع وعشرین وسبعمائة (Th. 192.) Æ ·5 Æ ·55

I.

No.	Mint: Date.	*Obv.*	*Rev.*
284–286	732	الملك والـعـظـمـة لله	عبد الراجی محمد تغلق ٧٣٢ (Th. 193.) Æ ·6 Æ ·55 Æ ·6

Æ No.	Mint: Date.	Obv.	Rev.
287	732	Same as 284.	Same as 284 : but date reversed, ٧٣٦ Æ ·6
288	733	„	„ but ٧٣٣ (Th. 193.) Æ ·6
289	734	„	„ ٧٣٤ (Th. 193.) Æ ·6
290	735	„	„ ٧٣٥ (Th. 193.) Æ ·65

K.

Æ No.	Mint: Date.	Obv.	Rev.
291–294	733	الراجى رحمة الله الكريم	محمد بن تغلق سنة ثلث وثلثين وسبعمائة (Th. 194.) Æ ·6 Æ ·6 Pl. V. Æ ·6 Æ ·6
295, 296	734	„	„ but اربع (Th. 194.) Æ ·6 Æ ·6

Æ No.	Mint: Date.	*Obv.*	*Rev.*
297, 297*a*	735	Same.	Same: but خمس (Th. 194.) Æ ·6 Æ ·6
298	737	„	„ but سبع (Th. 194.) Æ ·55

L.

Æ No.	Mint: Date.	*Obv.*	*Rev.*
299	734?	Same.	In centre, within double circle, محمد تغلق Margin, (؟) ..[ر]سی چہا .... Æ ·55

FORCED CURRENCY.

COPPER AND BRASS.

M.

Æ No.	Mint: Date.	
300–303	Dehlí 731	Obv. Area, within circle, من اطاع السلطان فقد اطاع الرحمن Margin,* در تخت گاه دهلی سال بر هفصد سی یك Rev. Area, مهر شد تنگة رائج در روزگار بنده امیدوار محمد تغلق (Th. 195.) Æ ·8 Pl. V. Æ ·8 Æ ·85 (Blundered.) Æ ·8
304, 305	,,	Same: omitting تخت گاه Æ ·8 Æ ·75

* The ت of هفتصد is uniformly omitted.

Æ No.	Mint: Date.	
305*a*	Dár al-Islám (Dehlí) 7*xx*	Same as 304. Margin, در دار الاسلام سال بر هفصد .... Æ ·8
305*b*	Agrah, 730?	Same. Margin, در اقره شهور سال بر هفصد سی (؟) Æ ·75
305*c*	Taghlak-púr 730	Same. Margin, فی اقلیم تغلقپور ... صث سال بر هفصد سی Æ ·8
305*d*	Satgáon 731	Same. Margin, در حضرت ستگانون سال ...د سی یک Æ ·8

N.

50-*Kání Piece.*

Æ No.	Mint: Date.	
306	Daulat-ábád 732?	Obv. Area as on 300. Margin, در تخت گاه دولتاباد سال بر هفصد سی دو (؟) Rev. Area as 300, but second line, پنچاه کانی در روزگار instead of رائج در روزگار (Th. 196.) Brass. ·8
307, 308		Same: date illegible. Brass. ·75 Æ ·85

Æ

O.

No.	Mint: Date.	*Obv.*	*Rev.*
309, 310	730	مــن اطــاع الـسلـطـان محمـد ٧٣٥	فــقد اطــاع الـرحـمـن تـغـلـق (Th. 197.) Æ ·75 Æ ·75

P.

No.	Mint: Date.	*Obv.*	*Rev.*
311, 312	730	اطيعـوا الـلـه واطـيعوا الرسول واولـى الامـر منكم محمد ٧٣٥	لا يولا السلطان كـل الـناس بعضهم بعضـا تغلق (Th. 198.) Æ ·75 Æ ·7
313	730	,, omitting ا after second اطيعو, and putting منكم in line with الامر	,, but arranged in three lines. Æ ·65

Q.

Quarter-'Adlí.

No.	Mint: Date.	*Obv.*	*Rev.*
314	730	ضرب الربعى ٧٣٥	محمد بن تـغـلـق (Th. 199.) Æ ·6
315	732	,, ٧٣٢	,, Æ ·6

Æ

No.	Mint: Date.	Obv.	Rev.
		R.	
316	730	حسبی ربی ۷۳۰	عبده تغلق محمد بن Pl. V. (Th. 200.) Æ ·55
317–317*b*		,, no ciphers.	محمد بن تغلق Æ ·6 Æ ·55 Æ ·7
		S.	
318		سکة زر جائز در عهد بندها میدوار ؟ [محمد تغلق]	Within double circle, محمد تغلق Around, श्रीः मोहमद *Sríḥ Mohamad* Pl. V. (Th. 201.*) Æ ·6

* Where سکة is erroneously read تنکة.

Æ

T.

No.	Mint: Date.	Obv.	Rev.
319	*Dár-al-Islám* (Dehlí) 730	ضرب الدرهم الشرعی فی زمن العبد محمد بن تغلق	بدار الاسلام فی سنة ثلثين وسبعمائة (Th. 202.) Æ ·65
320, 321	Dehlí 730	,, differently divided.	بحضرة دهلی فی سنة ثلثين وسبعمائة Pl. V. (Th. 203.) Æ ·65 Æ ·65
322	Dehlí 730	,,	,, but بدار الملك *vice* بحضرة, and differently divided. (Th. 202.) Æ

V.

8-*Kání Piece*.

No.	Mint: Date.	Obv.	Rev.
323		عدل کانی هشت	محمد تغلق (Th. 205.) Æ ·55

Æ

No.	Mint : Date.	Obv.	Rev.
		X.	
324	Dehlí	تغــلــق شــا (*sic*) محمد بن	دار الملك دهلی Æ ·6
		Y.	
325, 326	732	الملك والعزة لله	Within circle, محمــد تــغـلـق Around, سال بر هفصد سی دو Pl. V. (Th. 208.) Æ ·6 Æ ·6
		Z.	
327		السلطان ظل الله	محمد بن تـغـلـقشاه (Th. 209.) Æ ·6

No.	Mint: Date.	
		COINS STRUCK IN THE NAME OF THE 'ABBÁSÍ KHALÍFAHS OF EGYPT.
		I.—AL-MUSTAKFÍ II.
		A.H. 701—740.
AV		GOLD.
328	Dehlí 741	Obv. Area, within quatrefoil, ضرب هذا الدينار الخليفتى فى الدهلى فى شهور سنة احدى واربعين وسبعمائة Rev. Area, فى الزمان الامام المستكفى بالله امير المومنين ابو الربيع سليمان خلد الله خلافته PL. VI. (Th. 213.) *AV* ·9, Wt. 170
329	Dehlí 741	Same: but زمان, and خلد خلافته *AV* ·95, Wt. 171
330	Dehlí 74*x*	Same as 328: unit of date obscured by ornament. *AV* ·9, Wt. 166
331	Dehlí 743	Same: but ثلاث (Th. 212.) *AV* ·9, Wt. 170

COPPER.

Æ No.	Mint: Date.	*Obv.*	*Rev.*
332		الامام الاعظ[م خليفة الله فى العا[مين ...	Within circle, المستكفى بالله امير المو منين Margin illegible. (Th. 215*a*.) Æ ·75
333	743	خليفة الله فى شهور	المستكفى بالله ٧٤٣ Pl. VI. (Th. 214.) Æ ·6

II.—AL-HÁKIM.

A.H. 741—753.

GOLD.

No.	Mint: Date.	Obv.	Rev.
AV 334, 335		Within cinquefoil, فی زمان الامام امیر المومنین الحا کم بامر	Within cinquefoil, الله ابو العباس احمد خلد ملکه (Th. 213.) (I.O.C.) *Pierced.* AV ·8, Wt. 170

(No cinquefoils.) Pl. VI. AV ·85, Wt. 169

COPPER.

No.	Mint: Date.	Obv.	Rev.
Æ 336- 338		Within quatrefoil, احمد ا العباس بو	Within quatrefoil, الله الحاکم بامر Æ ·7 Pl. VI. Æ ·7 Æ ·65
339	748	ابو العباس احمد	,, at left, سنة ٧۴٨ Æ ·7

Small.

No.	Mint: Date.	Obv.	Rev.
340	748	,,	الحاکم بامر الله ٧۴٨ Æ ·5
341		Same as 336.	Same as 336. Æ ·5

No.	Mint: Date.	

MAHMÚD SHÁH.

IBN MUHAMMAD IBN TAGHLAK.

(*Pretender.*)

A.H. 752.

GOLD.

AV

342 Obv. Area,

يمين
امـــير المـومـنيـن
غياث الدنيا والدين
ابو المظفر

Rev. Area,

محـــــمــــود شـاه
بن محمد شاه بن
تغلقشاة السلطـــان
....

PL. VI. AV ·75, Wt. 169

No.	Mint: Date.	

XX.—FÍRÓZ SHÁH III.

A.H. 752—790.

Ꞥ GOLD.

343 Obv. Area,*

ضربت هذه السكة
فى زمان الامام
ابو العباس احمد
خلدت خلاف[ته

Rev. Area,

واثق بتائيد
يزدانى فيروز شاه
سلطانى

Pl. VI. (Th. 223.) Ꞥ ·8, Wt. 169

344 Obv. Area,†

ضربت هذه السكة
فى زمن الامام امير المومنين
ابى الفتح المعتضد بالله
خلد[ت] خلافته

Rev. Area,

السلطان الاعظم
سيف امير المومنين
ابو المظفر فيروز شاه
السلطانى خلدت مملكته

Pl. VI. (Th. 225.) Ꞥ ·8, Wt. 169

---

* The name of the khalífah Al-Hákim Abu-l-'Abbás Ahmad, combined with Fíróz Sháh's, probably limits the date of this coin to 752-3.

† Al-Mo'tadid was khalífah from 753 to 763.

AV No.	Mint: Date.	
345	Dehlí [7]5*x*	Obv. Area, within circle, فی زمن الامام امیر المومنین ابو الفتح خلدت خلافته Margin, ... دهلی سنة ... وخمسین .... Rev. as 344, but مملکته beneath السلطانی (*Cf.* Th. 224.) I. O. C. AV ·85 Wt. 167
346		Same : but margin illegible. AV ·9, Wt. 166
347	(Dehlí) 7*xx*	Obv. Area, within circle, فی زمن الامام امیر المومنین ابو الفتح خلدت خلافته Margin, ضربت هذه السکة بحضـ..........سن وسبعمائة Rev. as 345. (*Cf.* Th. 224.) AV ·9, Wt. 170
348	788	Obv. Area, سلطانی فیروز شاه Rev. Area, ا]لمومنین نائب امیر ۷۸۸ Pl. VI. (Th. 227.) AV ·75, Wt. 168

COPPER.

Æ No.	Mint: Date.	Obv.	Rev.
349	Dehlí 767	الخليفة امير المومنين خلدت خلافته ٧٦٧	فيروز شاه سلطانی ضربت بحضرت دهلی (Th. 228.) Æ ·75
350	Dehlí 770	,, ٧٧٥	,, (Th. 228.) Æ ·7
351	Dehlí 771	,, ٧٧١	,, (Th. 228.) Æ ·7
352	Dehlí 772	,, ٧٧٢	,, (Th. 228.) Æ ·7
353	Dehlí 773	,, ٧٧٣	,, Pl. VI. (Th. 228.) Æ ·7
354	Dehlí 776	,, ٧٧٦	,, (Th. 228.) Æ ·75
355	Dehlí 777	,, ٧٧٧	,, (Th. 228.) Æ ·7

Æ No.	Mint: Date.	Obv.	Rev.
356	Dehlí 778	Same as 349 : ۷۷۸	Same as 349. (Th. 228.) Æ ·7
357	Dehlí 780	„ ۷۸٠	„ (Th. 228.) Æ ·75
358, 358*a*	Dehlí 783	„ ۷۸۳	„ (Th. 228.) Æ ·7 Æ ·7
359	Dehlí 784	*ال]خليفة ابو عبد الله خلدت خلافته ۷۸۴	„ (Th. 228.) Æ ·75
360	Dehlí 786	Same as 349 : but ۷۸۶	„ (Th. 228.) Æ ·7
361	Dehlí 787	Same as 359 : but ۷۸۷	„ (*Cf.* Th. 230.) Æ ·7

* *I.e.* Al-Mutawakkil, A.H. 763—785.

Æ No.	Mint: Date.	Obv.	Rev.
362	Dehlí 788	Same as 359 : ٧٨٨	Same as 349. Æ ·7
363	Dehlí 789	,, ٧٨٩	,, Æ ·65
		(POSTHUMOUS.)	
364	Dehlí 816	Same as 349 : but ٨١٦	,, (Th. 238.) Æ ·7
365	Dehlí 817	,, ٨١٧	,, (Th. 238.) Æ ·7
		SMALL SIZE.	
366–368		Within sixfoil, احمد* العباس ابو	Within sixfoil, فیروز شاه سلطانی Pl. VI. (Th. 235.) Æ ·55 Æ ·6 Æ ·5
369, 370		الخليفة† ابو الفتح خلدت خلافته	فیروز شاه سلطانی خلد ملکه Pl. VI. (Th. 229.) Æ ·55 Æ ·55

* Al-Hákim: 740—753.

† Al-Mu'tadid: 753—763.

Æ No.	Mint: Date.	*Obv.*	*Rev.*
371	Dehlí	الخـــلـــيفة [امير المومنين خلدت خلافته	فـــيـــروز شاه سلطانى ضربت بحضرت دهلى (See above, 349.) Æ ·55
372	Dehlí 759	"	" Beneath, ٧٥٩ Æ ·55
373	Dehlí	الخـلـيفـة ابو عبد الـــلـ[ه خلدت خلاف[ته	" No date. (*Cf.* Th. 230.) Æ ·6
374–378	*Dar-al-Mulk.* Dehlí	دار الملك دهـــلـــى	فيروز شاه سلطـــانى Pl. VI. (Th. 233.) Æ ·6 Æ ·6 Æ ·6 Æ ·55 Æ ·55

(POSTHUMOUS.)

Æ No.	Mint: Date.	*Obv.*	*Rev.*
379	Dehlí 825	" Beneath, ٨٢٤	" (Th. 239.) Æ ·65
380	Dehlí	دهـــلـــى حضـــرت	سلـطـانى فـــيـــروز (Th. 234.) Æ ·55
381	Dehlí	حضـــرت دهـــلـــى	فـــيـــروز سلطـــانى Æ ·45

WITH FATḤ KHÁN.

COPPER.

No.	Mint: Date.	Obv.	Rev.
Æ			
382		فی زمن الامام امیر المومنین ا[بو ا]لفتح المعتضد بالل[ه .... خلاف[ته	شاه فتخان فیروز ج]ل الله ظلا[له و] جلا[له Pl. VI. (Th. 240.) Æ ·7
		Small.	
383		„ last lines, ابو الفتح خلدت خلافته	„ Pl. VI. Æ ·55
		Larger.	
384, 385		فی زمن الامام امیر المومنین ا[بو عبد الله خلدت خلافته	„ Æ ·7 (Th. 242.) Æ ·7
386	Dehlí	„	„ lower lines, ج]ل ظلال جلال ضربت دهل[ی Æ ·75

No.	Mint: Date.	WITH ẒAFAR.	
Æ		COPPER.	
		Obv.	*Rev.*
387	Dehlí 791 *Post-humous.*	الخـــليفة ابو عبد الله خلدت خلافتـه ۷۹۱	فــيــروز شـــاه ظفر سلطانی ضربت بحضرت دهلـــی (Th. 247.) Æ ·7
388		الخـــلـــيفـــة ابو عـبـد الـلـــه حـلـ . (*sic*) خـلـــدت خلاف[تـه	„ Pl. VI. Æ ·7
		Small.	
389, 390		الله ابو عـــبـــد خلدت خلافته	فيـــروز شـــاه ظـــفـر ابـــن فــيـــروز شاه Pl. VI. (Th. 248.) Æ ·6 Æ ·6
391, 392		الخليفة ابـو عبد الـلـ[ه خـلدت خلافته	فـــيـــروز شاه ظـفـر سـلـطـانـی (Th. 249.) Æ ·55 Æ ·5

No.	Mint: Date.

XXI.—GHIYÁS-AD-DÍN TAGHLAK SHÁH II.

A.H. 790—791.

COPPER.

No.	Mint: Date.	Obv.	Rev.
Æ			
393	Dehlí 790	ال]خليفة ابو عبد الله خلدت خلافته ٧٩٠	تغلق شاه سلطانی ضربت بحضرت دهلی PL. VII. (Th. 250.) Æ ·7
394, 395		الله ابو عبد خلدت خلافته	تغلق شاه سلطانی خلدت مملكته PL. VII. (*Cf.* Th. 252.) Æ ·65 Æ ·6
396, 397	*Dár-al-Mulk* Dehlí	دار الملك دهلی	تغلق شاه سلطانی (Th. 254.) Æ ·5 Æ ·6

XXII.—ABÚ-BAKR SHÁH.

A.H. 791—792.

COPPER.

No.	Mint: Date	Obv.	Rev.
Æ			
398	791	الخليفة ابو عبد الله خلدت خلافته ۷۹۱	ابو بكر شاه بن ظفر بن فيروز شاه سلطانى PL. VII. (Th. 255.) Æ ·7
399, 400	792	" ۷۹۲	" (Th. 255.) Æ ·75 Æ ·65
401	793	" ۷۹۳	" (Th. 255.) Æ ·7
402, 403	792	المومنين نائب امير ۷۹۲	Within square, شاه ابو بكر Around, ظفر بن فيروز شاه سلطانى PL. VII. (Th. 257.) Æ ·7 Æ ·7

Æ No.	Mint: Date.	Obv.	Rev.
404		Same as 402.	Within circle, بكر شاه ابو Margin, فيروز شاه .... (Th. 258.) Æ ·75
405	792	نائب امير المومنين خلدت خلافته ٧٩٢	ابو بكر شاه ظفر بن فيروز شاه سلطانى (Th. 259.) Æ ·8

Small.

Æ No.	Mint: Date.	Obv.	Rev.
406, 407		الخليفة ابو عبد الله خلدت خلافته	ا]بو بكر شاه ظفر سلطانى Pl. VII. (Th. 260.) Æ ·5 Æ ·55
408		الخليفة ا]مير المومنين خلدت خلافته	ا]بو بكر شاه بن ظفر بن فيروز شا[ه سلطانى Æ ·6
409		الله ابو عبد خلدت] خلاف[ته	اب]و [بكر شاه ظف[ر سلطانى Æ ·6

XXIII.—MUHAMMAD SHÁH III. IBN FÍRÓZ.

A.H. 792—798.

COPPER.

No.	Mint: Date.	Obv.	Rev.
Æ 410	Dehlí 790	In centre, الــــله عــبــد ابو Around, خلدت خلافته ضربت بحـضرت دهلی ۷۹۰	سلـــطـــانی فـــیروز شـــاه محـمــــد شاه Pl. VII. (Th. 261.) Æ ·85
411, 412	790	الخـلـيفـة ابـو عبد الله خلدت خـلافـتـه ۷۹۰	,, (Th. 265.) Æ ·75 Æ ·75
413, 414	793	,, ۷۹۳	,, (سلطانی for سلطان) (Th. 265.) Æ ·75 Æ ·7
415	794	,, ۷]۹۴	,, (سلطانی.) (Th. 265.) Æ ·7

Æ No.	Min : Date.	Obv.	Rev.
416	Dehlí 793	المومنين نائب امير ٧٩٣	Within circle, شاه محمد Around, ضربت حضرت دهلی .... Pl. VII. (Th. 266.) Æ ·7
417	794	,, ٧]٩٤	,, Mint obliterated. Æ ·7
418	*Dár-al-Mulk* Dehlí 793	دار الملك دهلی ٧٩٣	سلطانی محمد شاه Pl. VII. (Th. 267.) Æ ·55
419	Dehlí 794	,, ٧٩٤	,, (Th. 267.) Æ ·55
420, 420*a*		الخليفة ابو عبد الله]ه خلدت خلاف]ته	سلطان فيروز شا]ه محمد شاه (Th. 269 ?) Æ ·55 Æ ·55

Æ No.	Mint: Date.	POSTHUMOUS COINS.
		SILVER.
421	817	Obv. Area, فی زمن الامام ا]میر المومنین خلدت خلافته (*sic*) ۷۱۷ Rev. Area, السلطان [ا]لاعظم ا]بو المجاهد محمد شاه بن فیروز شاه سلطانی Pl. VII. (Th. 270.) Æ ·9, Wt. 174
422	818	Same: but ۸]۱۸ (Th. 270.) Æ ·85, Wt. 173
423		Same: but date obliterated. Æ ·9, Wt. 174

XXIV.—SIKANDAR SHÁH I.

A.H. 795.

COPPER.

No.	Mint: Date.	Obv.	Rev.
Æ			
424	795	الخليفة [ابو عبد الله خلد[ت خلافته ٧]٩٥	سلطانی محمد شاه سکندر شاه (Th. 272.) Æ ·7
425, 426	Dehlí 795	المومنين نائب امير ٧٩٤	In centre, شاه سکندر Around, ... بحضرت دهلی PL. VII. (Th. 273.) Æ ·65 Æ ·65
427, 428	*Dár-al-Mulk* Dehlí 795	دار الملك دهلی ٧٩٥	سلطانی سکندر شاه PL. VII. (Th. 274.) Æ ·6 Æ ·6
429, 430		ال]خليفة ا]مير المومنين خ]لدت خلا[فته	سلطانی محمد شاه سکن]در شاه بن Æ ·55 Æ ·5

No.	Mint: Date.	

XXV.—MAHMÚD SHÁH II.

A.H. 795—815.

GOLD.

No.	Mint: Date.	Obv.	Rev.
AV 431		فی زمن الامام امیر المومنین خلدت خلافته Traces of date beneath.	السلطان الاعظم ابو المظفر محمود شا]ه محمد شاه فیروز شا[اه سلطانی PL. VII. (Th. 276.) AV ·8, Wt. 171

SILVER.

No.	Mint: Date.	Obv.	Rev.
AR 432, 433		" Traces of date beneath.	" but ابو المجاهد AR ·9. Wt. 173 AR ·9, Wt. 173

COPPER.

No.	Mint: Date.	Obv.	Rev.
Æ 434	795	ا]لخليفة ابو عبد الله خلدت خلافته ٧٩٥	سلطانی محمد شاه محمود شاه PL. VII. (Th. 277.) Æ ·7

Æ

Small.

No.	Mint : Date.	*Obv.*	*Rev.*
435		الخـلـيـفـة امير المومنين خلـ[دت] خلاف[ته	Same as 434. (Th. 279.) Æ ·6
436–438	*Dár-al-Mulk* Dehlí 79*x*	دار الملك دهلى ۷۹[*x*	سلطانى محمود شاه Æ ·6 Æ ·5 Æ ·55
439	800	" ۸۰۰	" Pl. VII. (Th. 280.) Æ ·6
440	801	" ۸۰۱	" (Th. 280.) Æ ·55
441	815	" ۸۱۵	" Æ ·6

No.	Mint: Date.	Obv.	Rev.
		XXVI.—NASRAT SHÁH. (*Interregnum.*) A.H. 797 *ff.*	
		COPPER.	
Æ 442		المومنين امير نائب	سلطانی شاه نصرت (Th. 282.) Æ ·65
		Small.	
443	*Dár-al-Mulk* Dehlí 797	دار الملك دهلی ٧٩٧	شاه نصرت سلطانی Pl. VII. (Th. 284.) Æ ·6
444	798	" ٧٩٨	" (Th. 284.) Æ ·6
		POSTHUMOUS.*	
445	807	" ٨٠٧	" (Th. 285.) Æ ·6

* See nos. 364, 365, 379—381, for posthumous coins of Fírúz III. of years 816, 817, and 825; and nos. 421—423 for similar coins of Muhammad III. of 817 and 818.

No.	Mint: Date.	

FOURTH DYNASTY.

XXIX.—MUBÁRAK SHÁH II.

A H. 824—837.

COPPER.

No.	Mint: Date.	Obv.	Rev.
Æ			
446	(Dehlí) 835	المومنين نائب امير ٨٣٥	Within circle, شاه مبارك Around, ...ضت بحضر.... (Th. 288.) Æ ·8
447	Dehlí 83*x*	" ٨٣[*x*	Same centre: Around, سلطانی ضربت بحضرت دهلی Pl. VII. Æ ·8

Æ

Small.

No.	Mint : Date.	*Obv.*	*Rev.*
448	*Dár-al-Mulk* Dehlí 832	دار الملك دهلـــى ٨٣٢	مبارك شاه سلطـانى Pl. VII. (Th. 289.) Æ ·65
449	833	„ ٨٣٣	„ (Th. 289.) Æ ·6
450	834	„ ٨٣۴	„ (Th. 289.) Æ ·6
451	[8]34	„ ٨]٣۴	„ Æ ·65
452	835	„ ٨٣۵	„ (Th. 289.) Æ ·6
453	836	„ ٨٣٦	„ (Th. 289.) Æ ·6
454	837	„ ٨٣٧	„ (Th. 289.) Æ ·6
455	(Dehlí)	بحضرت	شـــاه مبـارك (Th. 290.) Æ ·5

XXX.—MUHAMMAD SHÁH IV. IBN FARÍD.

A.H. 837—847.

COPPER.

No.	Mint: Date.	Obv.	Rev.
Æ			
456	Dehlí 843	[ال]خليفة مير المومنين خلدت [خـ]لافته ٨٤٣	سلطان محمد شاه بن فرید شاه بحضرت دهلی (Th. 293.) Æ ·7
457	„ [8]46	„ ٩٦	„ Pl. VII. (Th. 293.) Æ ·75
458	„ [8]48	„ ٩٨	„ (Th. 293.) Æ ·75

Small.

No.	Mint: Date.	Obv.	Rev.
459		„ but خلدت خلافته in last line; and no date.	„ bottom line obliterated. Æ ·6

Æ No.	Mint: Date.	Obv.	Rev.
460	*Dár-al-Mulk* Dehlí 842,6, or 7	دار الملك دهلی ٨٤٠ (٨٤٢, ٦, or ٧)	محمد شاه سلطانی Pl. VII. (Th. 295.) Æ ·6
461	843	,, ٨٤٣	,, (Th. 295.) Æ ·6
462	844	,, ٨٤٤	,, (Th. 295.) Æ ·6
463	846?	,, ٨٤٦ (?)	,, (Th. 295.) Æ ·6
464	847	,, ٨٤٧	,, (Th. 295.) Æ ·6

Smaller.

Æ No.	Mint: Date.	Obv.	Rev.
465	8[4]3	,, ٨]٣٣ (*sic*)	,, Æ ·55

No.	Mint: Date.	*Obv.*	*Rev.*
466	*Dár-al-Mulk* (Dehlí)	Same as 460 : no date visible.	Same as 460. Æ ·55
467, 468		"	سلطان محمد شاه Æ ·55 Æ ·55
469	Dehlí	بحضرت دهلی	شاه محمد PL. VII. (Th. 296.) Æ ·45

XXXI.—'ÁLIM SHÁH.

A.H. 847—855.

COPPER.

No.	Mint: Date.	Obv.	Rev.
Æ			
470	Dehlí [8]53	الخـ]ـلـيـفـ[ـة امير المومنين خلـ]ـدت خـ]ـلافـتـه ٣٤[٨	سـلـطـان عـالـمـشـاه بـن محـمـد شـاه بحضر]ت د[هلى PL. VII. (Th. 297.) Æ ·7
		Small.	
471	*Dár-al-Mulk* Dehlí 853	دار الملك دهـلـى ٨٥٣	عـالمشاه سلطـان (Th. 300.) Æ ·55
472	[85]4	٤	,, PL. VII. (Th. 300.) Æ ·6

FIFTH DYNASTY.

XXXII.—BUHLÓL LÓDI.

A.H. 855—894.

COPPER.

No.	Mint: Date.	Obv.	Rev.
Æ 473	Dehlí 858	في زمن امير المومنيـــن خلد[ت خلافتـه ٨٤٨	المتـوكل على الرحمن بـهلول شاه سلـطـــان بحضرت دهـلى PL. VIII. (Th. 311.) Æ ·7
474	859	,, ٨٤٩	,, (Th. 311.) Æ ·7
475	860	,, ٨٦٥	,, (Th. 311.) Æ ·7
476	862	,, ٨٦٢	,, (Th. 311.) Æ ·7

Æ No.	Mint: Date.	*Obv.*	*Rev.*
477	Dehlí 884	Same as 473. ٨٨٤	Same as 473. Æ ·7
478	Dehlí 890	" ٨٩٠	" (Th. 311.) Æ ·65
479	877	ا]لمومنين نائب امير ٨]٧٧	Within circle, بهلـــول شـاه Around, ... السلطان (Th. 315.) Æ ·7
480	888	" ٨٨٨	" Margin illegible. Æ ·7
481	889	٨٨٩	" Margin obliterated. Æ ·65
482	890	" ٨٩٠	" Æ ·7

Æ

Small.

No.	Mint: Date.	Obv.	Rev.
483	*Dar-al-Mulk.* Dehlí 855	دار الملك دهلی ٨٤٤	بهلول شاه سلطان Pl. VIII. (Th. 313.) Æ ·65
484	857	„ ٧٤٧	„ Æ ·5
485	863	„ ٨٦٣	„ (Th. 313.) Æ ·6
486	863?	„ ٨٣٦ (= ٨٦٣?)	„ Æ ·6
487	867	„ ٨٦٧	„ (Th. 313.) Æ ·6
488	868	„ ٨٦٨	„ (Th. 313.) Æ ·55
489	873	„ ٨٧٣	„ (Th. 313.) Æ ·6
490	877	„ ٨٧٧	„ (Th. 313.) Æ ·5

Æ No.	Mint: Date.	*Obv.*	*Rev.*
491, 492	Dehlí	ا]لـخـلـيـــفـة امـيـر المومنين خلدت خلافة[ه	Same as 483. Beneath, بحضرت ده[لى (Th. 312.) Æ ·55 Æ ·55
		Large.	
493	Jaunpúr 888*	ساهـــه جـونپور ۸۸۸	بهلولشا ه سلطان Æ ·6
		Small.	
494	[8]93	" ۸]۹۳	" Two uncertain letters beneath. Æ ·5

* Date of final re-annexation of Jaunpúr.

XXXIII.—SIKANDAR II. LÓDI.

A.H. 894—923.

COPPER.

No.	Mint: Date.	Obv.	Rev.
Æ			
495	895	فی زمن امیر المومنین خلدت خلافته ٨٩٤	المتوکل [علی الرحمن سکندر شاه بهلول شاه سلطان (Th. 316.) Æ ·7
496	897 (or 6)	,, ٨٩٧ (or ٦ ?)	,, Æ ·65
497	898	,, ٨٩٨	,, Traces of words beneath ? * (Th. 316.) Æ ·65
498	902	,, ٩٠٢	,, Pl. VIII. (Th. 316.) Æ ·75
499	903	,, ٩٠٣	,, (Th. 316.) Æ ·75

* This is the only indication I can see on any of these coins of the possible presence on the die of the words بحضرت دهلی, described by Th., p. 366.

Æ No.	Mint: Date.	*Obv.*	*Rev.*
500, 501	906	Same as 495: ٩٠٦	Same as 495: (Th. 316.) Æ ·75 Æ ·7
502	907	" ٩٠٧ п	" (Th. 316.) Æ ·7
503	908	" ٩٠٨	" (Th. 316.) Æ ·7
504, 505	910	" ٩١٠	" 505, with star, and joined:— بهلولشا]ه (Th. 316.) Æ ·75 Æ ·75
506	911	" ٩١١	" No star or joining. (Th. 316.) Æ ·75
507, 508	914	" ٩١۴ п	" (Th. 316.) Æ ·7 Æ ·7
509, 510	915	" ٩١٥	" (Th. 316.) Æ ·8 Æ ·75

Æ No.	Mint: Date.	*Obv.*	*Rev.*
511	916	Same as 495: ٩١٦ ח	Same as 495: (Th. 316.) Æ ·7
512	917	,, with star ٩١٧	,, (Th. 316.) Æ ·7
513	918	,, ٩١٨	,, (Th. 316.) Æ ·75
514	919	,, ٩١٩	,, Star over ل of بهلول (Th. 316.) Æ ·75
515		,, Ciphers obscure.	,, No star. Æ ·75

Small.

Æ No.	Mint: Date.	*Obv.*	*Rev.*
516, 517		,, No ciphers. Partly cut off.	.... رحمن سكندر شـ[ـاه بهلول شـ[ـاه سلطـ[ـان Pl. VII. (Th. 317.) Æ ·55 Æ ·55

XXXIV.—IBRÁHÍM LÓDI.

A.H. 923—937.

COPPER.

No.	Mint: Date.	Obv.	Rev.
Æ			
518	926	فى] زمن المــومـنــيـــــن امير خلدت خلافته ٩٢٦	المتـ]وكل على ا]لرحمن ابراهيم شاه ســـكـــنــدر شـــاه سلطان (Cf. Th. 320.) Æ ·55
519		,, date obliterated.	,, Æ ·6
520		,, date obscure.	,, Æ ·6

(Thinner.)

No.	Mint: Date.	Obv.	Rev.
521–523	926	,, ٩٢٦	,, Æ ·5 Æ ·5 Æ ·5

(The inscriptions on the preceding six coins are extremely fragmentary.)

No. | Mint: Date.

SIXTH DYNASTY.

XXXV.—SHÉR SHÁH.

A.H. 946—952.

SILVER.

A. *Single Square Borders.*

a. With شير شاه arranged شاه / شير

Æ

524 | 946 | Obv. Area,

لا الـــه الا الله
محمد رسول الله
السلطان العادل

Margin, ابو بكر | عمر | عثمان | على

Rev. Area,

شـاه
شـيـر
السلطـــان خلد
الله ملكه ٩٤٦

श्री सेर साही
Ṣrí Ser Sáhí.

Margin, فريد | الدنيا | والدين | ابو المظفر

(Th. 351.) Æ 1·1, Wt. 175

525 | 946 | Same: but without line above شاه

Æ 1·1, Wt. 176

P

Æ

No.	Mint: Date.	
526	Sharíf- ábád 946	Same: Khalífahs' names run in a retrograde direction, علی | عثمان | عمر | ابو بکر Rev. Area, شاه شیر السلطان خلد الله ملکه شریفاباد ۹۴۶ श्री सेर साही Pl. VIII. (Th. 351.) Æ 1·05, Wt. 175
527	Sharíf- ábád 947	Same as 526: but date ۹۴۷ (Th. 351.) Æ 1·05, Wt. 176
528	948	Same as 524: but ۹۴۸ (Th. 351.) Æ 1·1, Wt. 174
529	949	Same as 524: but ۹۴۹ Æ 1·1, Wt. 172

---

b. With شاه شیر السلطان

Obv., same as 524:

No.	Mint: Date.	
530, 531	947 Jahán- panáh (Dehlí)	Rev. Area, شاه شیر السلطان خلد الله ملکه وسلطانه ۹۴۷ श्री सेर साही Margin [فر]ید الدنیا | والدین | ابو المظفر | جهانپناه (Cf. Th. 349*a*.) Æ 1·1, Wt. 175 Æ 1·05

AR No.	Mint : Date.	
532	Shér-garh ? 947	Same : but mint obscure : [شير]كر[ه] ? AR 1·05
533	948	Same as 530 : but date ٩٤٨ On rev., ⊞ AR 1·15, Wt. 173
534	Shér-garh ? 948	Same as 530 : but date ٩٤٨ and rev. margin, ... | . . . . . | ابو المظفر | ضرب شيركره (؟) AR 1·0, Wt. 171
535	Shérgarh 948	Same as 530 : but mint شيركره and date ٩٤٨ Obv. margin, بصدق ا[بى بكر] | بعدل ع[مر] | بحياى عثمان | بعلم على AR 1·05
536	Jahán-panáh (Dehlí) 949	Same as 530 : but date ٩٤٩ and rev. margin, فريد الدنيا | والدين | [ابو] المظفر | جهانپناه On rev., ⊞ AR 1·15, Wt. 177

B.

a. Within single Square Borders.

Æ No.	Mint : Date.	
537	Agrah 948	Obv. Area, لا الـــه الا الله محمد رسول الله Margin, با بكر الصديق | عمر الفاروق | عثمان العفان | على المرتضى Rev. Area, ٩۴ ٨ سـلـطـان شـيـر شـاه خلد الله ملكه श्री सार साह Margin, *Ṣrí Sár Sáha.* السلطان العادل | ابو المظفر فريد | الدنيا والدين | ضرب اگ[ر]ه Pl. VIII. (Cf. Th. 344.) Æ 1·1, Wt. 175
538	Agrah 949	Same : but ٩٤٩ sideways at left side of rev. ٩٤٩ ملكه Æ 1·15, Wt. 175
539, 540	Gwalior 951	Same : but ٩٥١ sideways at left side of rev. ; and ضرب گوالير instead of اكره (Th. 347.) Æ 1·1, Wt. 172 Æ 1·1
541	Gwalior 952	Same as 539, but ٩٥٢ Æ 1·1
542, 543	Shér- gadah	Areas similar to 537 : but without date. Obv. margin, ابا بكر صديق | عمر الخطاب | عثمان العفان | على المرتضى Rev. margin, فريد الدنيا و | الدين ابو المظفر | ضرب ش[ير] گده | [ش]ق بكره On rev., ✻ Æ 1·05, Wt. 175 Æ 1·1

(540, 541 and 542 read सेर)

Æ No.	Mint: Date.	
		b. Within double Square Borders.
544	Shér-garh 948	Obv. same as 537, but ابوبکر, and عثمان ذى النورين (instead of العفان) and a large ن over على Rev. Area, شاه شیر سلطـــان خلد الله ملکه Margin, ۹]۴۸ فرید الدنیا و | الدین ابو المظفر | ضرب شیرگره श्री सेर स PL. VIII. Æ 1·05, Wt. 178
545, 546	Shér-garh 9]49	Same: but ۴۹ On rev. of 545, * and [symbol] On obv. of 546, a sprig. (Th. 3:6.) Æ 1·1 Æ 1·1
547	Kálpí 949	Same: but beneath obv. area, * ضرب کالپی Nagari beneath rev. area, सेर सहि Rev. margin illegible except ابو المظفر (Th. 354.) Æ 1·05, Wt. 176

AR No.	Mint : Date.	C. *With circular areas.**
548	948	Obv. Area, لا الـــه الا الله محمد رسول الله Margin, ابا بكر عمر عسمان (*sic*) على السلطان العادل Rev. Area, شاه شير سلطـــان خلد الله ملكه وسلطانه Margin, فريد الدنيا والدين ابو المظفر श्री सेर साह ९४८ On obv., ❋ PL. VIII. (Th. 348.) AR 1·15, Wt. 174
549	949	Same: but ९४९, and عثمان (Th. 348.) AR 1·1
550	949	Same as 549 : but ابو بكر and date ९४९ at right side of Nagari. AR 1·1
551	Jahán-panáh (Dehlí) 949	Same as 549: but date ۹۴۹ in area under ملكه, and جهانپناه in margin after المظفر (Th. 349*a*.) AV 1·2, Wt. 175

* The margins of this type have generally one or two ornaments of a heart-shape, or in the form of a whorl, etc.

Æ No.	Mint : Date.	
552	950	Same as 550: but ۹۵۰ at right of Nagari. (Th. 348.) Æ 1·25
553	950	Same as 548 (عسمان): but ۹۵۰ at left of Nagari. Æ 1·25
554, 555	950	Same: but عثمان; and ۹۵۰ at left of Nagari. Æ 1·15 Æ 1·1
556	951	Same: but ۹۵۱ at left of Nagari. Æ 1·1
557	Sharíf-ábád 951	Same: but ۹۵۱ at right of Nagari, and شريفاباد beneath rev. area. Æ 1·1
558, 559	952	Same as 556: but ۹۵۲ at left of Nagari. Æ 1·2, Wt. 175 Æ 1·15

SQUARE SILVER.

		Obverse	Reverse
559a		لا الــــه الا الـلـه محمد رسول الله	السلطان شــــاه سير خلد الله ملكه स्रीसेरसाह

PL. VIII. *Square.* Æ ·75, Wt. 179

COPPER.*

Large.

Æ No.	Mint: Date.	*Obv.*	*Rev.*
560	949	فی عهد الامیر الحـامی الدین الدنان ۹۴۹	ابو المظفر شیر شاه السلطان خلد الله ملکه PL. VIII. (Cf. Th. 355.) Æ ·95
561, 562	950	" ۹٤٠	" Cf. Th. 355.) Æ ·95 Æ ·9
563, 564	951	" ۹٤۱	" (omitting الله) (Cf. Th. 355.) Æ ·95 Æ ·9
565	952	" ۹٤۲	" Æ ·95
566		" date obliterated.	" in centre, ✱ Æ ·9

* On the obv. the word الحامی is sometimes (566, 577, 579,) changed to الحاکمی ; and on other coins an intermediate form الحامی seems to be used. On the rev. of 561, 563, 577, 578, سلطان is substituted for السلطان.

Æ No.	Mint : Date	*Obv.*	*Rev.*
567	Agrah 950	Within square, فی عهد (*sic*) لامــــيــــر الحامی ٩٤٠ Outside, الدين الدنان السلطان العادل	Within square, سلطان شير شــــاه ضرب اگره Outside, ابو المظفر خلد الله [ملكه وسلطانه (Th. 356.) Æ ·95
568	950 or 1	„ ٩٤٠ or ٩٤١	„ but mint الور (?) Æ ·9
568*a*	Shér-garh 951	„ but ٩٤١ in margin.	„ mint شيرگره (Th. 368.) Æ 1·05
569	Hissár ? 951 ?	„ (?) in area ; marg. obscure.	„ حصار (Cf. Th. 357.) Æ ·95
570	Gwalior 950	„ ٩٤٠	„ گوالير marg. differently arranged. (Th. 358.) Æ ·95
571	Gwalior 951	„ ٩٤١	„ گوالير (Th. 358.) Æ ·95

Æ No.	Mint: Date.	Obv.	Rev.
572	Gwalior 952	Same as 567: ٩٤٢	Same as 571. (Th. 358.) Æ ·95
573	*x*	" date obliterated.	" but mint (?) حضرت Æ ·95
574	951	" no date in area; but ٩٤١ in margin.	Within square, سلطـــان شيـر شاه خلد الله Outside, ... وسلطان[ه]........... Æ 1·0
575		Within square, الامير الحامى فى عهد Margin varied.	Within square, السلطان غازى (؟) شير شــاه Margin, خلد الله مـ.......... Æ 1·0

Second Size.

Æ No.	Mint : Date.	*Obv.*	*Rev.*
576	948	فی عهد الامیر الحا]می الدین الدنیا]ن ۹]۴۸	ا]بو المظفر شیر شاه السلطان خلد ملکه Æ ·8
577	949	„ ۹۴۹	„ but سلطان ; and خلد الله ملکه Æ ·75
578	950	„ ۹۵۰	Same as 576: but سلطان Æ ·75
579	952	„ ۹۵۲	„ (السلطان) Æ ·85
580	952	„ ۹۵۲	„ Æ ·8

Æ No.	Mint : Date	Obv.	Rev.
581	Kálpí 945	Within square, فی عهد لامیر (*sic*) الحامی Margin, ... العادل ۹۴۵	Within square, سلطان شیر شاه ضرب کالپی Margin, ابو المظفر........... PL. VIII. Æ ·8
582	Kálpí	"	" Æ ·75
583		" blundered.	" mint obliterated. Æ ·8
584	Gwalior ?	السلطان العادل ابو المظفر شیر شاه .. سلطان	ا]لله خلد ملکه ضر]ب کوالیور؟ Æ ·8

Æ

Small

No.	Mint : Date.	*Obv.*	*Rev.*
585, 586	948	الــزمـــان خليــفـــة الــسـلـطـــان	سلطـــان شـــاه شـــيـــر الـعـــادل At side and beneath, [٩]٤٨ Æ ·5 Pl. VIII. Æ ·5
587, 588		"	" ciphers obliterated. Æ ·55 Æ ·5
589	94*x*	السلطان	" ٩٤*x* Æ ·55
590, 591		ا[لسلطا]ن ا[لزمـــان خـ]ـلـيـفـة (؟)	شـــاه شـــيـــر . . . . Pl. VIII. Æ ·4 Æ ·4

No. | Mint: Date.

XXXVI.—ISLÁM SHÁH.

A.H. 952—960.

SILVER.

Æ

A.

592 | 952 | Obv. Area, within square,

لا الــــه الا الله

محمد رسول الله

Margin, in segments,

ابا بكر الصديق | عمر الفاروق | عثمان العفان | على المرتضى

Rev. Area, within square,

اسلام شاه بن

شير شاه سلطان

خلد الله ملكه ٩٤٢

श्रीइसलामसाहि

Ṣrí Islám Sáhi

Margin, in segments,

السلطان العادل] جلال الد[نيا والدين] ابو المظفر

Æ 1·05, Wt. 168

593 | 952 | Same: but ٩٤٢ beneath obv. area, instead of at side of rev. area.

(Th. 360.) Æ 1·1, Wt. 173

Ꭿ No.	Mint : Date.		
594	Agrah 953	Same : but ۹۵۳ ; and mint, ضرب اگره Ornament on obv. area, ×	Ꭿ 1·15
595	Agrah 954	Same : but ۹۵۴. On obv. ✻, on rev. 卐	Ꭿ 1·05, Wt. 170
596	954	Same : ۹۵۴ ; rev. margin quite illegible. On obv. ✻	Ꭿ 1·05, Wt. 176
597	956	Same : but ۹۵۶ ; traces of mint in margin. On obv. ✻	PL. IX. Ꭿ 1·05
598	956	Same : ۹۵۶. On obv. ʒ.	Ꭿ 1·05
599, 600	Gwalior ? 957	Same : but ۹۵۷ ; margins illegible, except ضرب کولا... On obv. ه (*Ringed.*) On obv. د (Th. 360.)	Ꭿ 1·05 Ꭿ 1·0, Wt. 175
601	Gwalior 958	Same : but ۹۵۸. On obv. and rev., ه	Ꭿ ·95
602	960	Same : but ۹۶۰ ; margins illegible. On obv. ه	Ꭿ ·9
603		Same : but ≡ instead of ciphers. (Barbarous.)	Ꭿ 1·05

Æ No.	Mint : Date.	
		B.
604	952	Same as 592 : but ٩٥٢ horizontal ; and top segment of rev. margin, ٤٧٧ (ابن instead of بن) (Th. 359.) Æ 1·3, Wt. 172
605	953	Same : but ٩٥٣ (Th. 359.) Æ 1·3, Wt. 180
606	954	Same : but ٩٥٤ (Th. 359.) Æ 1·25, Wt. 166
607	955	Same : but ٩٥٥ (Th. 359.) Æ 1·25
608	957	Same : but ٩٥٧ Pl. IX. (Th. 359.) Æ 1·25, Wt. 175
609	958	Same : but ٩٥٨ (Th. 359.) Æ 1·25
610	959	Same : but ٩٥٩ (Th. 359.) Æ 1·3, Wt. 176
611	960	Same : but ٩٦٠ (Th. 359.) Æ 1·25
		C.
612	Gwalior ? 952	Same areas as 592 : but no date on rev. area. Obv. margin, ابا بكر وعمر | وعثمان | وعلى ضرب | كولاسر(؟) Rev. margin, السلطان العادل | ابو المظفر | [جلال] الدنيا والدين | سنة ٩٥٢ (ابن instead of بن) On rev. ✕ (Th. 360.) Æ 1·15, Wt. 17

AR No.	Mint: Date.	D.
613	Satgáon 955	Obv. Area, within square, لا اله الا الله محمد رسول الله ٩٥٥ Margin, in segments, ابا] بكر صديق | عمر خطاب | عثمان عفان | على مرتضى Rev. Area, within square, اسلام شاه ابن شير شاه سلطان خلد الله ملكه وسلطانه श्रीइसलामसाह Margin, in segments, retrograde, ضرب ستگانو | ابو المظفر | جلال الدنيا والدين PL. IX. (Th. 360.) AR 1·15, Wt. 176
		E.
614, 615	955	Same as 592 : but ٩٥٥ on obv. area. Rev. Area, اسلام شاه سلطان شير شاه خلد الله ملكه श्रीइसलामसाह Margin only partly legible. Ornament ✕ AR 1·1, Wt. 163 AR 1·1, Wt. 164
616, 617	956	Same as preceding, but ٩٥٦ on obv. area. Obv. margin of 616 as on 613 ; rev. margin differently arranged. Ornament on rev. ✕ AR 1·2 (*Clipped.*) AR ·9
618	956	Same as 592 : rev. margin illegible ; no ornament. AR 1·05

Æ No.	Mint: Date.	F.
619	957	Obv. Area, within double square, لا الـــه الا الـ]ه محمد رسول الله Margin, in segments (one only visible), موید (؟) الاسلام والمسـ]مین Rev. Area, within square, اسـام شـاه سـلـطـ]ـان (*sic*) بن شیر شاه سلطـ]ان خـلـد الـلـه مـلـكـه وسلطانه ٩٤٧[٩ Margin, in segments, illegible. (Very peculiar style.) PL. IX. Æ ·95, Wt. 162
		G.
620	954	Obv. Area, within circle, لا اله الا الله محمد رسول الله Margin, ابا بكر عمر عثمان على السلطان العادل Rev. Area, within circle, شـــاه اســـلام شیـر شـــاه سلطـــان خلد الله ملكه وسلطانه . . . . . (؟) Margin, جلال الدنيا والدين ابو المظفر | श्री इसलाम साहि ९५४ ✡ (Barbarous.) PL. IX. Æ 1·3, Wt. 175

Æ No.	Mint: Date.		

COPPER.

Thick and Large.

Æ No.	Mint: Date.	*Obv.*	*Rev.*
621	95*x*	فی عهد الامیر الحا]می الدین الدنان ۹٤	ابو المظفر اسلام شاه سلطان بن شیر شاه خلد الله ملکه (Th. 363.) Æ ·95
622	954	„ Beneath, ۹٤۴	Partly effaced. (Th. 363.) Æ ·9
623	960	„ (الحاکمی) Last line, ۹٦٠ [ا]لدین	اسلامشاه بن شیر شاه سلطان خلد الله ملکـ]ه Ornament, ꝏ Æ ·95

Second Size.

Æ No.	Mint: Date.	*Obv.*	*Rev.*
624	953	„ Date, in middle of last line, ۹٤۳	Same as 621. Æ ·8

Third Size.

Æ No.	Mint: Date.			
625		Within square, فی عهد ا]لامیر الحام[ی [الدین الدنان]	Within square, ا]سلامشاه شیر شاه سلطان	Æ ·65

Thin and Small.

Æ No.	Mint: Date.			
626–629		اسلام شاه شیر شاه سلطان	الزمان خلیفة العادل	(Th. 364.) Æ ·5 Æ ·5 Æ ·5 Æ ·5

Æ No.	Mint : Date.	

XXXVII.—MUHAMMAD 'ÁDIL SHÁH.

A.H. 960—964.

SILVER.

630, 631 | 961 | Obv. Area, within square,

لا الــه الا الله
محمد رسول الله

Margin, in segments,

ابا بكر الصديق | عمر الفاروق | عثمان العفان | علي المرتضى

Rev. Area, within square,

سلطان محمد عادل
خلد الله ملــكه
وسلطانه اعلى اجره
स्री सुल्तान मह
मद (in margin)
Srí Sultán Mahamad

Margin, in segments,

مبارز الدنيا والدين | ابو المظفر | ✡ | ٩٦١

Pl. IX. Æ 1·25, Wt. 164
Æ 1·3, Wt. 172

632 | Nárnól 961 | Same : but rev. area,

شــــاه سلطان
محمد عــــادل ٩٦١
خلد الله ملكه
श्रीमदमदसह
Ṣrí Mahamad Ṣah

Margin, ضرب نارنول | .... | .... | ....

Pl. IX. (Th. 365.) Æ 1·0, Wt. 177

633 | 963 | Same : but date ٩٦٣ ; and mint obscure.

(Th. 365.) Æ ·95, Wt. 159

COPPER.

Large.

Æ No.	Mint: Date.	Obv.	Rev.	
634, 635	961	فی عهد ا]لامیر الحامی ۹٦۱ الدین الدنیا[ن	ابو المجاه[د سلطان محمد شاه خلد الله ملکه	(Th. 366.) Æ ·9 Æ ·9

Small.

Æ No.	Mint: Date.	Obv.	Rev.	
636		,, no date visible.	ابو الم . . . . محمد ※ شاه	Æ ·7
637		,,	سلطا[ن] محمد خلد ※ ا[لله ملکه	Æ ·7

Æ No.	Mint : Date.	Obv.	Rev.
638	962 or 963	Same as 634 : beneath, date, ٩٦٢	مجا]هد (؟) الد . . محمد ※ شاه . . . . . . (Th. 366.) Æ ·7
639		„ no date visible.	مجا]هد . . . . . سل]طا[ن] محمد عادل خلد] ا ※ لله م[لكه Pl. IX. Æ ·7

XXXIX.—SIKANDAR SHÁH III.

A.H. 962.

SILVER.

Æ		
640	962	Obv. Area, within square, لا الـــه الا الله محمد رسول الله In segments, ... | ... عثمان عمر ابن خطاب | .... Rev. Area, سلطان سكندر شاه اسماسور عماب ٩٦٢ Margin, in segments, illegible. Pl. IX. Æ 1·0, Wt. 174

COPPER.

Æ No.	Mint : Date.	Obv.	Rev.
641		شاه سلطان سكندر	سلطان سكندر شاه PL. IX. (Cf. Th. 370.) Æ ·5
642		Illegible.	شاه سكندر سلطان Æ ·5

INDEXES.

8

I. INDEX OF YEARS.

A.H.	Metal.	MINT.	PRINCE.	NO.	Page.
695	AR	Dehlí	Ibráhím I.	153	37
,,	,,	,,	Muhammad I.	164, 165	39
697	,,	[,,]	,,	166	40
698	AV	,,	,,	157	38
699	AR	[,,]	,,	167	40
700	Æ	*x*	,,	182	41
701	,,	*x*	,,	183-185, 195	41, 42
702	,,	*x*	,,	186, 196	41, 42
703	AR	Dehlí	,,	168	40
,,	Æ	*x*	,,	197	42
704	AV	,,	,,	158	39
,,	Æ	*x*	,,	187	41
705	AR	Dehlí	,,	169	40
,,	Æ	*x*	,,	188	42
706?	,,	*x*	,,	189	42
708	AV	*Dár-al-Islám* [Dehli]	,,	159	39
710	,,	Dehlí	,,	160	39
,,	AR	[,,]	,,	170, 171	40
,,	Æ	*x*	,,	190	42
711	AR	*Dár-al-Islám* [Dehlí]	,,	172	40
,,	,,	Dehlí	,,	173	40
,,	Æ	*x*	,,	191	42
712	AR	Dehlí	,,	174	40
,,	Æ	*x*	,,	198	42
713	AR	Dehlí	,,	175, 176	40
,,	,,	*Dár-al-Islám* [Dehlí]	,,	177	41
,,	Æ	*x*	,,	199	43
714	AR	Dehlí	,,	178, 179	41
,,	Æ	*x*	,,	200	43
715	AV	[Dehlí]	,,	161	39
,,	AR	,,	,,	180	41
,,	Æ	*x*	,,	201	43
,,	,,	*x*	'Umár	205	43
716	AR	Dehlí	Mubárak I.	209, 210	45
,,	Æ	*x*	,,	214, 215	46
717	AR	Dehlí	,,	211	45
,,	,,	*Dár-al-Mulk* [Dehlí]	,,	212, 213	45
,,	Æ	*x*	,,	216-218, 221, 222	46, 47
718	AV	*Dár-al-Khiláfeh* [Dehlí]	,,	206	44
,,	AR	,,	,,	208	44
,,	Æ	*x*	,,	225, 226	47
719	AV	*Dár-al-Khiláfeh* [Dehlí]	,,	207	44
,,	Æ	*x*	,,	219, 220, 227, 229	46-48
720	,,	*x*	,,	228, 230-232	47, 48

A.H.	Metal.	MINT.	PRINCE.	NO.	Page.
720	AV	Dehlí	Khusrú	235	49
,,	Æ	x	,,	236	49
,,	AV	Dehlí	Taghlak I.	238	50
721	AR	Deógír	,,	243	52
,,	,,	x	,,	244	52
,,	Æ	x	,,	249, 250, 255	53, 54
722	AV	Dehlí	,,	239	51
,,	AR	,,	,,	245	52
,,	Æ	x	,,	251	53
723	AR	Dehlí	,,	246	52
,,	Æ	x	,,	252	53
724	AV	Dehlí	,,	240	51
,,	AR	,,	,,	247	52
,,	Æ	x	,,	253	53
725	AR	Dehlí	,,	248	52
,,	Æ	x	,,	254, 256	53, 54
,,	AR	Dehlí	Muhammad ibn Taghlak	263	55
,,	Æ	x	,,	278, 279	59
726	AV	,,	Taghlak I., *posthumous*	241	51
,,	,,	,,	Muhammad ibn Taghlak	260-262	55
,,	Æ	x	,,	280	60
727	AV	Dehlí	,,	264	56
,,	Æ	x	,,	281-283	60
728	AR	x	,,	268,269	57
729	AV	x	,,	265	56
,,	AR	x	,,	270,271	57
730	,,	x	,,	272	57
,,	,,	Sátgáon	,,	274	58
,,?	Æ	Agrah	,,	305*b*	64
,,	,,	Taghlakpúr	,,	305*c*	64
,,	,,	x	,,	309-314, 316-317*b*	65, 66
,,	,,	*Dár-al-Islám* [Dehlí]	,,	319	67
,,	,,	Dehlí	,,	320-322	67
731	,,	,,	,,	300-305	63
,,	,,	Sátgáon	,,	305*d*	64
732	,,	x	,,	284-287, 315,325-6	60,61, 65,68
,,?	,,	Daulatábád	,,	306	64
733	AV	x	,,	266,267	57
,,	Æ	x	,,	288, 291-294	61
734	,,	x	,,	289, 295, 296	61
,,?	,,	x	,,	299	62
735	,,	x	,,	290, 297	61, 62

A.H.	Metal.	MINT.	PRINCE.	NO.	Page.
911	Æ	*x*	Sikandar II.	506	102
914	,,	*x*	,,	507, 508	102
915	,,	*x*	,,	509, 510	102
916	,,	*x*	,,	511	103
917	,,	*x*	,,	512	103
918	,,	*x*	,,	513	103
919	,,	*x*	,,	514	103
926	,,	*x*	,,	518, 521-523	104
945	Æ	Kálpí	Shér Sháh	581	116
946	AR	*x*	,,	524, 525	105
,,	,,	Sharífábád	,,	526	106
947	,,	,,	,,	527	106
,,	,,	*Jahánpanáh* (Dehlí)	,,	530, 531	106
,,	,,	Shérgarh ?	,,	532	107
948	,,	*x*	,,	528, 533, 548	106, 107, 110
,,	,,	Shérgarh	,,	534, 535, 544	107, 109
,,	,,	Agrah	,,	537	108
,,	Æ	*x*	,,	576, 585, 586	115, 117
949	AR	*x*	,,	529, 549, 550	106, 110
,,	,,	*Jahánpanáh* (Dehlí)	,,	536, 551	107, 110
,,	,,	Agrah	,,	538	108
,,	,,	Shérgarh	,,	545, 546	109
,,	,,	Kálpí	,,	547	109
,,	Æ	*x*	,,	560, 577	112, 115
94*x*	,,	*x*	,,	589	117
950	AR	*x*	,,	552-555	111
,,	Æ	*x*	,,	561, 562, 578	112, 115
,,	,,	Agrah	,,	567	113
,,	,,	Gwalior	,,	570	113
95?	,,	Narnól ?	,,	568	113
951	AR	Gwalior	,,	539, 540	108
,,	,,	*x*	,,	556	111
,,	,,	Sharífábád	,,	557	111
,,	Æ	*x*	,,	563, 564, 574	112, 114
,,	,,	Shérgarh	,,	568*a*	113
,,	,,	Gwalior	,,	571	113
,, ?	,,	Hissár ?	,,	569	113
952	AR	Gwalior	,,	541	108
,,	,,	*x*	,,	558, 559	111
,,	Æ	*x*	,,	565, 579, 580	112, 115

A.H.	Metal.	MINT.	PRINCE.	NO.	Page.
952	Æ	Gwalior	Shér Sháh	572	114
,,	AR	*x*	Islám Sháh	592, 593, 604	118, 120
,,	,,	Gwalior	,,	612	120
953	,,	Agrah	,,	594	119
,,	,,	*x*	,,	605	120
,,	Æ	*x*	,,	624	123
954	AR	Agrah	,,	595	119
,,	,,	*x*	,,	596, 606, 620	119,120, 122
,,	Æ	*x*	,,	622	123
955	AR	*x*	,,	607, 614, 615	120, 121
,,	,,	Sátgáon	,,	613	121
956	,,	*x*	,,	597, 598, 616-618	119, 121
957	,,	Gwalior ?	,,	599, 600	119
,,	,,	*x*	,,	608, 619	120, 122
958	,,	Gwalior	,,	601	119
,,	,,	*x*	,,	609	120
959	,,	*x*	,,	610	120
95*x*	Æ	*x*	,,	621	123
960	AR	*x*	,,	602, 611	119, 120
,,	Æ	*x*	,,	623	123
961	AR	*x*	Muhammad 'Ádil	630, 631	125
,,	,,	Nárnól	,,	632	125
,,	Æ	*x*	,,	634, 635	126
962	AR	*x*	Sikandar III.	640	127
96$\frac{2}{3}$	Æ	*x*	Muhammad 'Ádil	638	126
963	AR	*x*	,,	633	125

Imperfect dates on nos. 181, 305*a*, 347.

II. INDEX OF MINTS.

MINT.	Metal.	A.H.	PRINCE.	NO.	Page.
دهلی *	Æ	x	Muhammad ibn Sám	12-16	9
Dehlí * *	"	x	Altamsh	38-42	15
	"	x	"	54,55	16
*	AR	x	Bahrám	67	19
	"	639-40	Mas'úd	73	21
	"	654	Mahmúd	86	25
	"	655	"	87	25
	"	657	"	88, 89	25
	"	658	"	90	25
	"	660	"	91	25
	"	662	"	92	26
	"	664	"	93	26
	"	"	Balbán	103-105	28
	"	665	"	106	28
	"	667	"	107	29
	"	669	"	108, 109	29
	AV	672	"	100	27
	AR	673	"	110	29
	"	674	"	111	29
	AV	675	"	101	27
	"	678	"	102	27
	AR	x	"	112-114	29
	"	686	Kai-Kubád	124,125	32
	AV	687	"	123	31
	AR	"	"	126	32
	"	688	"	127	32
	"	x	"	128	32
	"	68[9]	Fíróz II.	139	35
	"	690	"	140, 141	35
	"	691	"	142	35
	"	693	"	143	35
	"	694	"	144	36
	AV	695	"	138	34
	AR	"	"	145	36
	Æ	x	"	152, 152*a*	36
	AR	695	Ibráhím I.	153	37
	"	"	Muhammad I.	164, 165	39
	AV	698	"	157	38
	"	704	"	158	39
	AR	705	"	169	40
	AV	710	"	160	39

* An asterisk is prefixed to those coins which are only presumably Dehlí, the name itself being either obliterated, or else altogether absent. The epithet حضرت or حضرة (see note p. 35) is always prefixed to the name Dehlí, except in the thirty-five instances in which Dár-al-Mulk is prefixed, here indicated by D; and in no. 386, where Dehlí occurs with no prefix, and 328-331, where it is written الدهلی, and 300-305, where the Persian forms دردهلی or در تخت گاه are used.

MINT.	Metal.	A.H.	PRINCE.	NO.	Page.
شريفاباد Sharífábád	AR	946	Shér Sháh	526	106
	,,	947	,,	527	106
	,,	951	,,	557	111
شيرگده Shérgadah	AR	*x*	Shér Sháh	542, 543	108
شيرگره Shérgarh	AR	947	Shér Sháh	532	107
	,,	948	,,	534, 535, 544	107, 109
	,,	[9]49	,,	545, 546	109
	Æ	951	,,	568*a*	113
غـزنـة (بلدة)	AR	596	Muhammad ibn Sám	1	5
Ghazní (بلد)	,,	,,	,,	2	6
(بلدة)	AV	602	,,	6	8
,,	,,	603	,,	7	8
,,	,,	604	,,	8	9
	AR	$60\frac{3}{6}$	Yildiz	20	10
	,,	610	,,	21	10
قلعة *Kal'ah*			*See* ديوگير *Deógír*		
كالپى Kálpí	Æ	945	Shér Sháh	581	116
	AR	949	,,	547	109
	Æ	*x*	,,	582	116
[Kanauj]	AV	*x*	Muhammad ibn Sám	30-33	12

* Also written گولاير and گواليور.

III. INDEX OF NAMES.

س

ف

ق

ك

م

ن

و

ى

IV. INDEX OF NAGARI INSCRIPTIONS.

अ

स or श

V. INDEX OF POINTS, ORNAMENTS, AND BORDERS.

VI. INDEX OF DENOMINATIONS, MARKS AND FORMULAS OF GENUINENESS, ETC.

VII. INDEX OF FIGURES.

VIII. MISCELLANEOUS INDEX.

TABLE

OF THE

RELATIVE WEIGHTS OF

ENGLISH GRAINS and FRENCH GRAMMES.

Grains	Grammes.	Grains.	Grammes.	Grains.	Grammes.	Grains.	Grammes.
1	·064	41	2·656	81	5·248	121	7·840
2	·129	42	2·720	82	5·312	122	7·905
3	·194	43	2·785	83	5·378	123	7·970
4	·259	44	2·850	84	5·442	124	8·035
5	·324	45	2·915	85	5·508	125	8·100
6	·388	46	2·980	86	5·572	126	8·164
7	·453	47	3·045	87	5·637	127	8·229
8	·518	48	3·110	88	5·702	128	8·294
9	·583	49	3·175	89	5·767	129	8·359
10	·648	50	3·240	90	5·832	130	8·424
11	·712	51	3·304	91	5·896	131	8·488
12	·777	52	3·368	92	5·961	132	8·553
13	·842	53	3·434	93	6·026	133	8·618
14	·907	54	3·498	94	6·091	134	8·682
15	·972	55	3·564	95	6·156	135	8·747
16	1·036	56	3·628	96	6·220	136	8·812
17	1·101	57	3·693	97	6·285	137	8·877
18	1·166	58	3·758	98	6·350	138	8·942
19	1·231	59	3·823	99	6·415	139	9·007
20	1·296	60	3·888	100	6·480	140	9·072
21	1·360	61	3·952	101	6·544	141	9·136
22	1·425	62	4·017	102	6·609	142	9·200
23	1·490	63	4·082	103	6·674	143	9·265
24	1·555	64	4·146	104	6·739	144	9·330
25	1·620	65	4·211	105	6·804	145	9·395
26	1·684	66	4·276	106	6·868	146	9·460
27	1·749	67	4·341	107	6·933	147	9·525
28	1·814	68	4·406	108	6·998	148	9·590
29	1·879	69	4·471	109	7·063	149	9·655
30	1·944	70	4·536	110	7·128	150	9·720
31	2·008	71	4·600	111	7·192	151	9·784
32	2·073	72	4·665	112	7·257	152	9·848
33	2·138	73	4·729	113	7·322	153	9·914
34	2·202	74	4·794	114	7·387	154	9·978
35	2·267	75	4·859	115	7·452	155	10·044
36	2·332	76	4·924	116	7·516	156	10·108
37	2·397	77	4·989	117	7·581	157	10·173
38	2·462	78	5·054	118	7·646	158	10·238
39	2·527	79	5·119	119	7·711	159	10·303
40	2·592	80	5·184	120	7·776	160	10·368

TABLE

OF THE

RELATIVE WEIGHTS OF

ENGLISH GRAINS and FRENCH GRAMMES.

Grains.	Grammes.	Grains.	Grammes.	Grains.	Grammes.	Grains.	Grammes.
161	10·432	201	13·024	241	15·616	290	18·79
162	10·497	202	13·089	242	15·680	300	19·44
163	10·562	203	13·154	243	15·745	310	20·08
164	10·626	204	13·219	244	15·810	320	20·73
165	10·691	205	13·284	245	15·875	330	21·38
166	10·756	206	13·348	246	15·940	340	22·02
167	10·821	207	13·413	247	16·005	350	22·67
168	10·886	208	13·478	248	16·070	360	23·32
169	10·951	209	13·543	249	16·135	370	23·97
170	11·016	210	13·608	250	16·200	380	24·62
171	11·080	211	13·672	251	16·264	390	25·27
172	11·145	212	13·737	252	16·328	400	25·92
173	11·209	213	13·802	253	16·394	410	26·56
174	11·274	214	13·867	254	16·458	420	27·20
175	11·339	215	13·932	255	16·524	430	27·85
176	11·404	216	13·996	256	16·588	440	28·50
177	11·469	217	14·061	257	16·653	450	29·15
178	11·534	218	14·126	258	16·718	460	29·80
179	11·599	219	14·191	259	16·783	470	30·45
180	11·664	220	14·256	260	16·848	480	31·10
181	11·728	221	14·320	261	16·912	490	31·75
182	11·792	222	14·385	262	16·977	500	32·40
183	11·858	223	14·450	263	17·042	510	33·04
184	11·922	224	14·515	264	17·106	520	33·68
185	11·988	225	14·580	265	17·171	530	34·34
186	12·052	226	14·644	266	17·236	540	34·98
187	12·117	227	14·709	267	17·301	550	35·64
188	12·182	228	14·774	268	17·366	560	36·28
189	12·247	229	14·839	269	17·431	570	36·93
190	12·312	230	14·904	270	17·496	580	37·58
191	12·376	231	14·968	271	17·560	590	38·23
192	12·441	232	15·033	272	17·625	600	38·88
193	12·506	233	15·098	273	17·689	700	45·36
194	12·571	234	15·162	274	17·754	800	51·84
195	12·636	235	15·227	275	17·819	900	58·32
196	12·700	236	15·292	276	17·884	1000	64·80
197	12·765	237	15·357	277	17·949	2000	129·60
198	12·830	238	15·422	278	18·014	3000	194·40
199	12·895	239	15·487	279	18·079	4000	259·20
200	12·960	240	15·552	280	18·144	5000	324·00

TABLE

FOR

CONVERTING ENGLISH INCHES INTO MILLIMÈTRES

AND THE

MEASURES OF MIONNET'S SCALE.

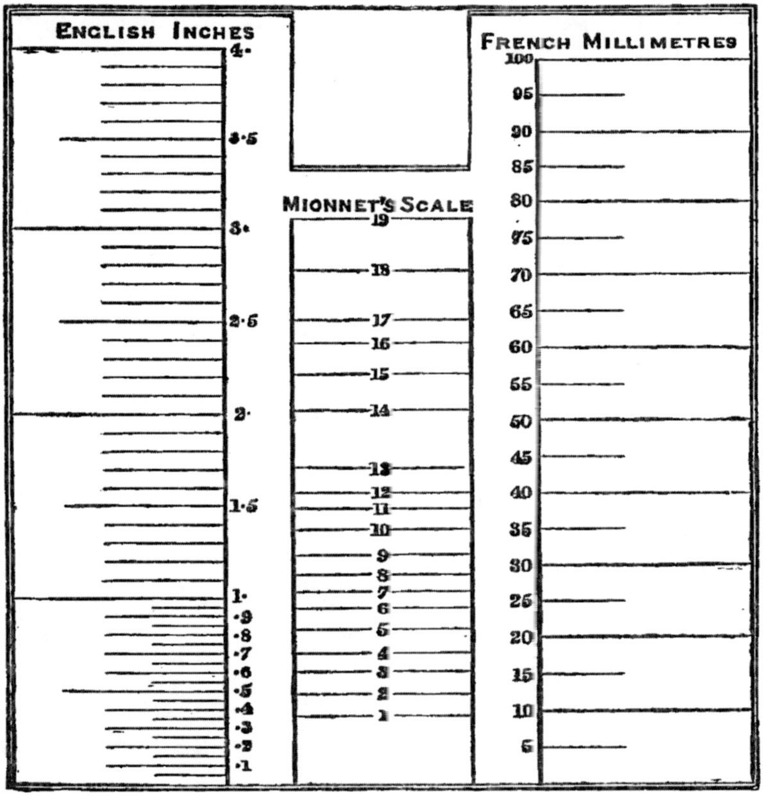

London: Gilbert & Rivington, Limited, St. John's Sq., Clerkenwell Road.

COMPARATIVE TABLE OF THE YEARS OF THE HIJRAH AND OF THE CHRISTIAN ERA.

A.H.	A.D.		A.H.	A.D.	
1	622 . .	July 16	51	671 . .	Jan. 18
2	623 . .	,, 5	52	672 . .	,, 8
3	624 . .	June 24	53	672 . .	Dec. 27
4	625 . .	,, 13	54	673 . .	,, 16
5	626 . .	,, 2	55	674 . .	,, 6
6	627 . .	May 23	56	675 . .	Nov. 25
7	628 . .	,, 11	57	676 . .	,, 14
8	629 . .	,, 1	58	677 . .	,, 3
9	630 . .	April 20	59	678 . .	Oct. 23
10	631 . .	,, 9	60	679 . .	,, 13
11	632 . .	Mar. 29	61	680 . .	,, 1
12	633 . .	,, 18	62	681 . .	Sept. 20
13	634 . .	,, 7	63	682 . .	,, 10
14	635 . .	Feb. 25	64	683 . .	Aug. 30
15	636 . .	,, 14	65	684 . .	,, 18
16	637 . .	,, 2	66	685 . .	,, 8
17	638 . .	Jan. 23	67	686 . .	July 28
18	639 . .	,, 12	68	687 . .	,, 18
19	640 . .	,, 2	69	688 . .	,, 6
20	640 . .	Dec. 21	70	689 . .	June 25
21	641 . .	,, 10	71	690 . .	,, 15
22	642 . .	Nov. 30	72	691 . .	,, 4
23	643 . .	,, 19	73	692 . .	May 23
24	644 . .	,, 7	74	693 . .	,, 13
25	645 . .	Oct. 28	75	694 . .	,, 2
26	646 . .	,, 17	76	695 . .	April 21
27	647 . .	,, 7	77	696 . .	,, 10
28	648 . .	Sept. 25	78	697 . .	Mar. 30
29	649 . .	,, 14	79	698 . .	,, 20
30	650 . .	,, 4	80	699 . .	,, 9
31	651 . .	Aug. 24	81	700 . .	Feb. 26
32	652 . .	,, 12	82	701 . .	,, 15
33	653 . .	,, 2	83	702 . .	,, 4
34	654 . .	July 22	84	703 . .	Jan. 24
35	655 . .	,, 11	85	704 . .	,, 14
36	656 . .	June 30	86	705 . .	,, 2
37	657 . .	,, 19	87	705 . .	Dec. 23
38	658 . .	,, 9	88	706 . .	,, 12
39	659 . .	May 29	89	707 . .	,, 1
40	660 . .	,, 17	90	708 . .	Nov. 20
41	661 . .	,, 7	91	709 . .	,, 9
42	662 . .	April 26	92	710 . .	Oct. 29
43	663 . .	,, 15	93	711 . .	,, 19
44	664 . .	,, 4	94	712 . .	,, 7
45	665 . .	Mar. 24	95	713 . .	Sept. 26
46	666 . .	,, 13	96	714 . .	,, 16
47	667 . .	,, 3	97	715 . .	,, 5
48	668 . .	Feb. 20	98	716 . .	Aug. 25
49	669 . .	,, 9	99	717 . .	,, 14
50	670 . .	Jan. 29	100	718 . .	,, 3

A.H.	A.D.		A.H.	A.D.	
101	719	July 24	151	768	Jan. 26
102	720	,, 12	152	769	,, 14
103	721	,, 1	153	770	,, 4
104	722	June 21	154	770	Dec. 24
105	723	,, 10	155	771	,, 13
106	724	May 29	156	772	,, 2
107	725	,, 19	157	773	Nov. 21
108	726	,, 8	158	774	,, 11
109	727	April 28	159	775	Oct. 31
110	728	,, 16	160	776	,, 19
111	729	,, 5	161	777	,, 9
112	730	Mar. 26	162	778	Sept. 28
113	731	,, 15	163	779	,, 17
114	732	,, 3	164	780	,, 6
115	733	Feb. 21	165	781	Aug. 26
116	734	,, 10	166	782	,, 15
117	735	Jan. 31	167	783	,, 5
118	736	,, 20	168	784	July 24
119	737	,, 8	169	785	,, 14
120	737	Dec. 29	170	786	,, 3
121	738	,, 18	171	787	June 22
122	739	,, 7	172	788	,, 11
123	740	Nov. 26	173	789	May 31
124	741	,, 15	174	790	,, 20
125	742	,, 4	175	791	,, 10
126	743	Oct. 25	176	792	April 28
127	744	,, 13	177	793	,, 18
128	745	,, 3	178	794	,, 7
129	746	Sept. 22	179	795	Mar. 27
130	747	,, 11	180	796	,, 16
131	748	Aug. 31	181	797	,, 5
132	749	,, 20	182	798	Feb. 22
133	750	,, 9	183	799	,, 12
134	751	July 30	184	800	,, 1
135	752	,, 18	185	801	Jan. 20
136	753	,, 7	186	802	,, 10
137	754	June 27	187	802	Dec. 30
138	755	,, 16	188	803	,, 20
139	756	,, 5	189	804	,, 8
140	757	May 25	190	805	Nov. 27
141	758	,, 14	191	806	,, 17
142	759	,, 4	192	807	,, 6
143	760	April 22	193	808	Oct. 25
144	761	,, 11	194	809	,, 15
145	762	,, 1	195	810	,, 4
146	763	Mar. 21	196	811	Sept. 23
147	764	,, 10	197	812	,, 12
148	765	Feb. 27	198	813	,, 1
149	766	,, 16	199	814	Aug. 22
150	767	,, 6	200	815	,, 11

A.H.	A.D.	
201	816	July 30
202	817	,, 20
203	818	,, 9
204	819	June 28
205	820	,, 17
206	821	,, 6
207	822	May 27
208	823	,, 16
209	824	,, 4
210	825	April 24
211	826	,, 13
212	827	,, 2
213	828	Mar. 22
214	829	,, 11
215	830	Feb. 28
216	831	,, 18
217	832	,, 7
218	833	Jan. 27
219	834	,, 16
220	835	,, 5
221	835	Dec. 26
222	836	,, 14
223	837	,, 3
224	838	Nov. 23
225	839	,, 12
226	840	Oct. 31
227	841	,, 21
228	842	,, 10
229	843	Sept. 30
230	844	,, 18
231	845	,, 7
232	846	Aug. 28
233	847	,, 17
234	848	,, 5
235	849	July 26
236	850	,, 15
237	851	,, 5
238	852	June 23
239	853	,, 12
240	854	,, 2
241	855	May 22
242	856	,, 10
243	857	April 30
244	858	,, 19
245	859	,, 8
246	860	Mar. 28
247	861	,, 17
248	862	,, 7
249	863	Feb. 24
250	864	,, 13

A.H.	A.D.	
251	865	Feb. 2
252	866	Jan. 22
253	867	,, 11
254	868	,, 1
255	868	Dec. 20
256	869	,, 9
257	870	Nov. 29
258	871	,, 18
259	872	,, 7
260	873	Oct. 27
261	874	,, 16
262	875	,, 6
263	876	Sept. 24
264	877	,, 13
265	878	,, 3
266	879	Aug. 23
267	880	,, 12
268	881	,, 1
269	882	July 21
270	883	,, 11
271	884	June 29
272	885	,, 18
273	886	,, 8
274	887	May 28
275	888	,, 16
276	889	,, 6
277	890	April 25
278	891	,, 15
279	892	,, 3
280	893	Mar. 23
281	894	,, 13
282	895	,, 2
283	896	Feb. 19
284	897	,, 8
285	898	Jan. 28
286	899	,, 17
287	900	,, 7
288	900	Dec. 26
289	901	,, 16
290	902	,, 5
291	903	Nov. 24
292	904	,, 13
293	905	,, 2
294	906	Oct. 22
295	907	,, 12
296	908	Sept. 30
297	909	,, 20
298	910	,, 9
299	911	Aug. 29
300	912	,, 18

A.H.	A.D.		A.H.	A.D.	
301	913 . .	Aug. 7	351	962 . .	Feb. 9
302	914 . .	July 27	352	963 . .	Jan. 30
303	915 . .	,, 17	353	964 . .	,, 19
304	916 . .	,, 5	354	965 . .	,, 7
305	917 . .	June 24	355	965 . .	Dec. 28
306	918 . .	,, 14	356	966 . .	,, 17
307	919 . .	,, 3	357	967 . .	,, 7
308	920 . .	May 23	358	968 . .	Nov. 25
309	921 . .	,, 12	359	969 . .	,, 14
310	922 . .	,, 1	360	970 . .	,, 4
311	923 . .	April 21	361	971 . .	Oct. 24
312	924 . .	,, 9	362	972 . .	,, 12
313	925 . .	Mar. 29	363	973 . .	,, 2
314	926 . .	,, 19	364	974 . .	Sept. 21
315	927 . .	,, 8	365	975 . .	,, 10
316	928 . .	Feb. 25	366	976 . .	Aug. 30
317	929 . .	,, 14	367	977 . .	,, 19
318	930 . .	,, 3	368	978 . .	,, 9
319	931 . .	Jan. 24	369	979 . .	July 29
320	932 . .	,, 13	370	980 . .	,, 17
321	933 . .	,, 1	371	981 . .	,, 7
322	933 . .	Dec. 22	372	982 . .	June 26
323	934 . .	,, 11	373	983 . .	,, 15
324	935 . .	Nov. 30	374	984 . .	,, 4
325	936 . .	,, 19	375	985 . .	May 24
326	937 . .	,, 8	376	986 . .	,, 13
327	938 . .	Oct. 29	377	987 . .	,, 3
328	939 . .	,, 18	378	988 . .	Apr. 21
329	940 . .	,, 6	379	989 . .	,, 11
330	941 . .	Sept. 26	380	990 . .	Mar. 31
331	942 . .	,, 15	381	991 . .	,, 20
332	943 . .	,, 4	382	992 . .	,, 9
333	944 . .	Aug. 24	383	993 . .	Feb. 26
334	945 . .	,, 13	384	994 . .	,, 15
335	946 . .	,, 2	385	995 . .	,, 5
336	947 . .	July 23	386	996 . .	Jan. 25
337	948 . .	,, 11	387	997 . .	,, 14
338	949 . .	,, 1	388	998 . .	,, 3
339	950 . .	June 20	389	998 . .	Dec. 23
340	951 . .	,, 9	390	999 . .	,, 13
341	952 . .	May 29	391	1000 . .	,, 1
342	953 . .	,, 18	392	1001 . .	Nov. 20
343	954 . .	,, 7	393	1002 . .	,, 10
344	955 . .	April 27	394	1003 . .	Oct. 30
345	956 . .	,, 15	395	1004 . .	,, 18
346	957 . .	,, 4	396	1005 . .	,, 8
347	958 . .	Mar. 25	397	1006 . .	Sept. 27
348	959 . .	,, 14	398	1007 . .	,, 17
349	960 . .	,, 3	399	1008 . .	,, 5
350	961 . .	Feb. 20	400	1009 . .	Aug. 25

A.H.	A.D.		A.H.	A.D.	
401	1010 . .	Aug. 15	451	1059 . .	Feb. 17
402	1011 . .	,, 4	452	1060 . .	,, 6
403	1012 . .	July 23	453	1061 . .	Jan. 26
404	1013 . .	,, 13	454	1062 . .	,, 15
405	1014 . .	,, 2	455	1063 . .	,, 4
406	1015 . .	June 21	456	1063 . .	Dec. 25
407	1016 . .	,, 10	457	1064 . .	,, 13
408	1017 . .	May 30	458	1065 . .	,, 3
409	1018 . .	,, 20	459	1066 . .	Nov. 22
410	1019 . .	,, 9	460	1067 . .	,, 11
411	1020 . .	April 27	461	1068 . .	Oct. 31
412	1021 . .	,, 17	462	1069 . .	,, 20
413	1022 . .	,, 6	463	1070 . .	,, 9
414	1023 . .	Mar. 26	464	1071 . .	Sept. 29
415	1024 . .	,, 15	465	1072 . .	,, 17
416	1025 . .	,, 4	466	1073 . .	,, 6
417	1026 . .	Feb. 22	467	1074 . .	Aug. 27
418	1027 . .	,, 11	468	1075 . .	,, 16
419	1028 . .	Jan. 31	469	1076 . .	,, 5
420	1029 . .	,, 20	470	1077 . .	July 25
421	1030 . .	,, 9	471	1078 . .	,, 14
422	1030 . .	Dec. 29	472	1079 . .	,, 4
423	1031 . .	,, 19	473	1080 . .	June 22
424	1032 . .	,, 7	474	1081 . .	,, 11
425	1033 . .	Nov. 26	475	1082 . .	,, 1
426	1034 . .	,, 16	476	1083 . .	May 21
427	1035 . .	,, 5	477	1084 . .	,, 10
428	1036 . .	Oct. 25	478	1085 . .	April 29
429	1037 . .	,, 14	479	1086 . .	,, 18
430	1038 . .	,, 3	480	1087 . .	,, 8
431	1039 . .	Sept. 23	481	1088 . .	Mar. 27
432	1040 . .	,, 11	482	1089 . .	,, 16
433	1041 . .	Aug. 31	483	1090 . .	,, 6
434	1042 . .	,, 21	484	1091 . .	Feb. 23
435	1043 . .	,, 10	485	1092 . .	,, 12
436	1044 . .	July 29	486	1093 . .	,, 1
437	1045 . .	,, 19	487	1094 . .	Jan. 21
438	1046 . .	,, 8	488	1095 . .	,, 11
439	1047 . .	June 28	489	1095 . .	Dec. 31
440	1048 . .	,, 16	490	1096 . .	,, 19
441	1049 . .	,, 5	491	1097 . .	,, 9
442	1050 . .	May 26	492	1098 . .	Nov. 28
443	1051 . .	,, 15	493	1099 . .	,, 17
444	1052 . .	,, 3	494	1100 . .	,, 6
445	1053 . .	April 23	495	1101 . .	Oct. 26
446	1054 . .	,, 12	496	1102 . .	,, 15
447	1055 . .	,, 2	497	1103 . .	,, 5
448	1056 . .	Mar. 21	498	1104 . .	Sept. 23
449	1057 . .	,, 10	499	1105 . .	,, 13
450	1058 . .	Feb. 28	500	1106 . .	,, 2

A.H.	A.D.		A.H.	A.D.	
501	1107 . .	Aug. 22	551	1156 . .	Feb. 25
502	1108 . .	,, 11	552	1157 . .	,, 13
503	1109 . .	July 31	553	1158 . .	,, 2
504	1110 . .	,, 20	554	1159 . .	Jan. 23
505	1111 . .	,, 10	555	1160 . .	,, 12
506	1112 . .	June 28	556	1160 . .	Dec. 31
507	1113 . .	,, 18	557	1161 . .	,, 21
508	1114 . .	,, 7	558	1162 . .	,, 10
509	1115 . .	May 27	559	1163 . .	Nov. 30
510	1116 . .	,, 16	560	1164 . .	,, 18
511	1117 . .	,, 5	561	1165 . .	,, 7
512	1118 . .	April 24	562	1166 . .	Oct. 28
513	1119 . .	,, 14	563	1167 . .	,, 17
514	1120 . .	,, 2	564	1168 . .	,, 5
515	1121 . .	Mar. 22	565	1169 . .	Sept. 25
516	1122 . .	,, 12	566	1170 . .	,, 14
517	1123 . .	,, 1	567	1171 . .	,, 4
518	1124 . .	Feb. 19	568	1172 . .	Aug. 23
519	1125 . .	,, 7	569	1173 . .	,, 12
520	1126 . .	Jan. 27	570	1174 . .	,, 2
521	1127 . .	,, 17	571	1175 . .	July 22
522	1128 . .	,, 6	572	1176 . .	,, 10
523	1128 . .	Dec. 25	573	1177 . .	June 30
524	1129 . .	,, 15	574	1178 . .	,, 19
525	1130 . .	,, 4	575	1179 . .	,, 8
526	1131 . .	Nov. 23	576	1180 . .	May 28
527	1132 . .	,, 12	577	1181 . .	,, 17
528	1133 . .	,, 1	578	1182 . .	,, 7
529	1134 . .	Oct. 22	579	1183 . .	April 26
530	1135 . .	,, 11	580	1184 . .	,, 14
531	1136 . .	Sept. 29	581	1185 . .	,, 4
532	1137 . .	,, 19	582	1186 . .	Mar. 24
533	1138 . .	,, 8	583	1187 . .	,, 13
534	1139 . .	Aug. 28	584	1188 . .	,, 2
535	1140 . .	,, 17	585	1189 . .	Feb. 19
536	1141 . .	,, 6	586	1190 . .	,, 8
537	1142 . .	July 27	587	1191 . .	Jan. 29
538	1143 . .	,, 16	588	1192 . .	,, 18
539	1144 . .	,, 4	589	1193 . .	,, 7
540	1145 . .	June 24	590	1193 . .	Dec. 27
541	1146 . .	,, 13	591	1194 . .	,, 16
542	1147 . .	,, 2	592	1195 . .	,, 6
543	1148 . .	May 22	593	1196 . .	Nov. 24
544	1149 . .	,, 11	594	1197 . .	,, 13
545	1150 . .	April 30	595	1198 . .	,, 3
546	1151 . .	,, 20	596	1199 . .	Oct. 23
547	1152 . .	,, 8	597	1200 . .	,, 12
548	1153 . .	Mar. 29	598	1201 . .	,, 1
549	1154 . .	,, 18	599	1202 . .	Sept. 20
550	1155 . .	,, 7	600	1203 . .	,, 10

A.H.	A.D.	
601	1204 . .	Aug. 29
602	1205 . .	" 18
603	1206 . .	" 8
604	1207 . .	July 28
605	1208 . .	" 16
606	1209 . .	" 6
607	1210 . .	June 25
608	1211 . .	" 15
609	1212 . .	" 3
610	1213 . .	May 23
611	1214 . .	" 13
612	1215 . .	" 2
613	1216 . .	April 20
614	1217 . .	" 10
615	1218 . .	Mar. 30
616	1219 . .	" 19
617	1220 . .	" 8
618	1221 . .	Feb. 25
619	1222 . .	" 15
620	1223 . .	" 4
621	1224 . .	Jan. 24
622	1225 . .	" 13
623	1226 . .	" 2
624	1226 . .	Dec. 22
625	1227 . .	" 12
626	1228 . .	Nov. 30
627	1229 . .	" 20
628	1230 . .	" 9
629	1231 . .	Oct. 29
630	1232 . .	" 18
631	1233 . .	" 7
632	1234 . .	Sept. 26
633	1235 . .	" 16
634	1236 . .	" 4
635	1237 . .	Aug. 24
636	1238 . .	" 14
637	1239 . .	" 3
638	1240 . .	July 23
639	1241 . .	" 12
640	1242 . .	" 1
641	1243 . .	June 21
642	1244 . .	" 9
643	1245 . .	May 29
644	1246 . .	" 19
645	1247 . .	" 8
646	1248 . .	April 26
647	1249 . .	" 16
648	1250 . .	" 5
649	1251 . .	Mar. 26
650	1252 . .	" 14
651	1253 . .	Mar. 3
652	1254 . .	Feb. 21
653	1255 . .	" 10
654	1256 . .	Jan. 30
655	1257 . .	" 19
656	1258 . .	" 8
657	1258 . .	Dec. 29
658	1259 . .	" 18
659	1260 . .	" 6
660	1261 . .	Nov. 26
661	1262 . .	" 15
662	1263 . .	" 4
663	1264 . .	Oct. 24
664	1265 . .	" 13
665	1266 . .	" 2
666	1267 . .	Sept. 22
667	1268 . .	" 10
668	1269 . .	Aug. 31
669	1270 . .	" 20
670	1271 . .	" 9
671	1272 . .	July 29
672	1273 . .	" 18
673	1274 . .	" 7
674	1275 . .	June 27
675	1276 . .	" 15
676	1277 . .	" 4
677	1278 . .	May 25
678	1279 . .	" 14
679	1280 . .	" 3
680	1281 . .	April 22
681	1282 . .	" 11
682	1283 . .	" 1
683	1284 . .	Mar. 20
684	1285 . .	" 9
685	1286 . .	Feb. 27
686	1287 . .	" 16
687	1288 . .	" 6
688	1289 . .	Jan. 25
689	1290 . .	" 14
690	1291 . .	" 4
691	1291 . .	Dec. 24
692	1292 . .	" 12
693	1293 . .	" 2
694	1294 . .	Nov. 21
695	1295 . .	" 10
696	1296 . .	Oct. 30
697	1297 . .	" 19
698	1298 . .	" 9
699	1299 . .	Sept. 28
700	1300 . .	" 16

A.H.	A.D.		A.H.	A.D.	
701	1301	. . Sept. 6	751	1350	. . Mar. 11
702	1302	. . Aug. 26	752	1351	. . Feb. 28
703	1303	. . ,, 15	753	1352	. . ,, 18
704	1304	. . ,, 4	754	1353	. . ,, 6
705	1305	. . July 24	755	1354	. . Jan. 26
706	1306	. . ,, 13	756	1355	. . ,, 16
707	1307	. . ,, 3	757	1356	. . ,, 5
708	1308	. . June 21	758	1356	. . Dec. 25
709	1309	. . ,, 11	759	1357	. . ,, 14
710	1310	. . May 31	760	1358	. . ,, 3
711	1311	. . ,, 20	761	1359	. . Nov. 23
712	1312	. . ,, 9	762	1360	. . ,, 11
713	1313	. . April 28	763	1361	. . Oct. 31
714	1314	. . ,, 17	764	1362	. . ,, 21
715	1315	. . ,, 7	765	1363	. . ,, 10
716	1316	. . Mar. 26	766	1364	. . Sept. 28
717	1317	. . ,, 16	767	1365	. . ,, 18
718	1318	. . ,, 5	768	1366	. . ,, 7
719	1319	. . Feb. 22	769	1367	. . Aug. 28
720	1320	. . ,, 12	770	1368	. . ,, 16
721	1321	. . Jan. 31	771	1369	. . ,, 5
722	1322	. . ,, 20	772	1370	. . July 26
723	1323	. . ,, 10	773	1371	. . ,, 15
724	1323	. . Dec. 30	774	1372	. . ,, 3
725	1324	. . ,, 18	775	1373	. . June 23
726	1325	. . ,, 8	776	1374	. . ,, 12
727	1326	. . Nov. 27	777	1375	. . ,, 2
728	1327	. . ,, 17	778	1376	. . May 21
729	1328	. . ,, 5	779	1377	. . ,, 10
730	1329	. . Oct. 25	780	1378	. . April 30
731	1330	. . ,, 15	781	1379	. . ,, 19
732	1331	. . ,, 4	782	1380	. . ,, 7
733	1332	. . Sept. 22	783	1381	. . Mar. 28
734	1333	. . ,, 12	784	1382	. . ,, 17
735	1334	. . ,, 1	785	1383	. . ,, 6
736	1335	. . Aug. 21	786	1384	. . Feb. 24
737	1336	. . ,, 10	787	1385	. . ,, 12
738	1337	. . July 30	788	1386	. . ,, 2
739	1338	. . ,, 20	789	1387	. . Jan. 22
740	1339	. . ,, 9	790	1388	. . ,, 11
741	1340	. . June 27	791	1388	. . Dec. 31
742	1341	. . ,, 17	792	1389	. . ,, 20
743	1342	. . ,, 6	793	1390	. . ,, 9
744	1343	. . May 26	794	1391	. . Nov. 29
745	1344	. . ,, 15	795	1392	. . ,, 17
746	1345	. . ,, 4	796	1393	. . ,, 6
747	1346	. . April 24	797	1394	. . Oct. 27
748	1347	. . ,, 13	798	1395	. . ,, 16
749	1348	. . ,, 1	799	1396	. . ,, 5
750	1349	. . Mar. 22	800	1397	. . Sept. 24

A.H.	A.D.		A.H.	A.D.	
801	1398	Sept. 13	851	1447	Mar. 19
802	1399	„ 3	852	1448	„ 7
803	1400	Aug. 22	853	1449	Feb. 24
804	1401	„ 11	854	1450	„ 14
805	1402	„ 1	855	1451	„ 3
806	1403	July 21	856	1452	Jan. 23
807	1404	„ 10	857	1453	„ 12
808	1405	June 29	858	1454	„ 1
809	1406	„ 18	859	1454	Dec. 22
810	1407	„ 8	860	1455	„ 11
811	1408	May 27	861	1456	Nov. 29
812	1409	„ 16	862	1457	„ 19
813	1410	„ 6	863	1458	„ 8
814	1411	April 25	864	1459	Oct. 28
815	1412	„ 13	865	1460	„ 17
816	1413	„ 3	866	1461	„ 6
817	1414	Mar. 23	867	1462	Sept. 26
818	1415	„ 13	868	1463	„ 15
819	1416	„ 1	869	1464	„ 3
820	1417	Feb. 13	870	1465	Aug. 24
821	1418	„ 3	871	1466	„ 13
822	1419	Jan. 28	872	1467	„ 2
823	1420	„ 17	873	1468	July 22
824	1421	„ 6	874	1469	„ 11
825	1421	Dec. 26	875	1470	June 30
826	1422	„ 15	876	1471	„ 20
827	1423	„ 5	877	1472	„ 8
828	1424	Nov. 23	878	1473	May 29
829	1425	„ 13	879	1474	„ 18
830	1426	„ 2	880	1475	„ 7
831	1427	Oct. 22	881	1476	April 26
832	1428	„ 11	882	1477	„ 15
833	1429	Sept. 30	883	1478	„ 4
834	1430	„ 19	884	1479	Mar. 25
835	1431	„ 9	885	1480	„ 13
836	1432	Aug. 28	886	1481	„ 2
837	1433	„ 18	887	1482	Feb. 20
838	1434	„ 7	888	1483	„ 9
839	1435	July 27	889	1484	Jan. 30
840	1436	„ 16	890	1485	„ 18
841	1437	„ 5	891	1486	„ 7
842	1438	June 24	892	1486	Dec. 28
843	1439	„ 14	893	1487	„ 17
844	1440	„ 2	894	1488	„ 5
845	1441	May 22	895	1489	Nov. 25
846	1442	„ 12	896	1490	„ 14
847	1443	„ 1	897	1491	„ 4
848	1444	April 20	898	1492	Oct. 23
849	1445	„ 9	899	1493	„ 12
850	1446	Mar. 29	900	1494	„ 2

A.H.	A.D.	
901	1495 . .	Sept. 21
902	1496 . .	,, 9
903	1497 . .	Aug. 30
904	1498 . .	,, 19
905	1499 . .	,, 8
906	1500 . .	July 28
907	1501 . .	,, 17
908	1502 . .	,, 7
909	1503 . .	June 26
910	1504 . .	,, 14
911	1505 . .	,, 4
912	1506 . .	May 24
913	1507 . .	,, 13
914	1508 . .	,, 2
915	1509 . .	April 21
916	1510 . .	,, 10
917	1511 . .	Mar. 31
918	1512 . .	,, 19
919	1513 . .	,, 9
920	1514 . .	Feb. 26
921	1515 . .	,, 15
922	1516 . .	,, 5
923	1517 . .	Jan. 24
924	1518 . .	,, 13
925	1519 . .	,, 3
926	1519 . .	Dec. 23
927	1520 . .	,, 12
928	1521 . .	,, 1
929	1522 . .	Nov. 20
930	1523 . .	,, 10
931	1524 . .	Oct. 29
932	1525 . .	,, 18
933	1526 . .	,, 8
934	1527 . .	Sept. 27
935	1528 . .	,, 15
936	1529 . .	,, 5
937	1530 . .	Aug. 25
938	1531 . .	,, 15
939	1532 . .	,, 3
940	1533 . .	July 23
941	1534 . .	,, 13
942	1535 . .	,, 2
943	1536 . .	June 20
944	1537 . .	,, 10
945	1538 . .	May 30
946	1539 . .	,, 19
947	1540 . .	,, 8
948	1541 . .	April 27
949	1542 . .	,, 17
950	1543 . .	,, 6
951	1544 . .	Mar. 25
952	1545 . .	,, 15
953	1546 . .	,, 4
954	1547 . .	Feb. 21
955	1548 . .	,, 11
956	1549 . .	Jan. 30
957	1550 . .	,, 20
958	1551 . .	,, 9
959	1551 . .	Dec. 29
960	1552 . .	,, 18
961	1553 . .	,, 7
962	1554 . .	Nov. 26
963	1555 . .	,, 16
964	1556 . .	,, 4
965	1557 . .	Oct. 24
966	1558 . .	,, 14
967	1559 . .	,, 3
968	1560 . .	Sept. 22
969	1561 . .	,, 11
970	1562 . .	Aug. 31
971	1563 . .	,, 21
972	1564 . .	,, 9
973	1565 . .	July 29
974	1566 . .	,, 19
975	1567 . .	,, 8
976	1568 . .	June 26
977	1569 . .	,, 16
978	1570 . .	,, 5
979	1571 . .	May 26
980	1572 . .	,, 14
981	1573 . .	,, 3
982	1574 . .	April 23
983	1575 . .	,, 12
984	1576 . .	Mar. 31
985	1577 . .	,, 21
986	1578 . .	,, 10
987	1579 . .	Feb. 28
988	1580 . .	,, 17
989	1581 . .	,, 5
990	1582 . .	Jan. 26
991	1583 . .	,, 25*
992	1584 . .	,, 14
993	1585 . .	,, 3
994	1585 . .	Dec. 23
995	1586 . .	,, 12
990	1587 . .	,, 2
997	1588 . .	Nov. 20
998	1589 . .	,, 10
999	1590 . .	Oct. 30
1000	1591 . .	,, 19

* Here the change to the Gregorian New Style occurs.

A.H.	A.D.		A.H.	A.D.	
1001	1592 . .	Oct. 8	1051	1641 . .	April 12
1002	1593 . .	Sept. 27	1052	1642 . .	„ 1
1003	1594 . .	„ 16	1053	1643 . .	Mar. 22
1004	1595 . .	„ 6	1054	1644 . .	„ 10
1005	1596 . .	Aug. 25	1055	1645 . .	Feb. 27
1006	1597 . .	„ 14	1056	1646 . .	„ 17
1007	1598 . .	„ 4	1057	1647 . .	„ 6
1008	1599 . .	July 24	1058	1648 . .	Jan. 27
1009	1600 . .	„ 13	1059	1649 . .	„ 15
1010	1601 . .	„ 2	1060	1650 . .	„ 4
1011	1602 . .	June 21	1061	1650 . .	Dec. 25
1012	1603 . .	„ 11	1062	1651 . .	„ 14
1013	1604 . .	May 30	1063	1652 . .	„ 2
1014	1605 . .	„ 19	1064	1653 . .	Nov. 22
1015	1606 . .	„ 9	1065	1654 . .	„ 11
1016	1607 . .	April 28	1066	1655 . .	Oct. 31
1017	1608 . .	„ 17	1067	1656 . .	„ 20
1018	1609 . .	„ 6	1068	1657 . .	„ 9
1019	1610 . .	Mar. 26	1069	1658 . .	Sept. 29
1020	1611 . .	„ 16	1070	1659 . .	„ 18
1021	1612 . .	„ 4	1071	1660 . .	„ 6
1022	1613 . .	Feb. 21	1072	1661 . .	Aug. 27
1023	1614 . .	„ 11	1073	1662 . .	„ 16
1024	1615 . .	Jan. 31	1074	1663 . .	„ 5
1025	1616 . .	„ 20	1075	1664 . .	July 25
1026	1617 . .	„ 9	1076	1665 . .	„ 14
1027	1617 . .	Dec. 29	1077	1666 . .	„ 4
1028	1618 . .	„ 19	1078	1667 . .	June 23
1029	1619 . .	„ 8	1079	1668 . .	„ 11
1030	1620 . .	Nov. 26	1080	1669 . .	„ 1
1031	1621 . .	„ 16	1081	1670 . .	May 21
1032	1622 . .	„ 5	1082	1671 . .	„ 10
1033	1623 . .	Oct. 25	1083	1672 . .	April 29
1034	1624 . .	„ 14	1084	1673 . .	„ 18
1035	1625 . .	„ 3	1085	1674 . .	„ 7
1036	1626 . .	Sept. 22	1086	1675 . .	Mar. 28
1037	1627 . .	„ 12	1087	1676 . .	„ 16
1038	1628 . .	Aug. 31	1088	1677 . .	„ 6
1039	1629 . .	„ 21	1089	1678 . .	Feb. 23
1040	1630 . .	„ 10	1090	1679 . .	„ 12
1041	1631 . .	July 30	1091	1680 . .	„ 2
1042	1632 . .	„ 19	1092	1681 . .	Jan. 21
1043	1633 . .	„ 8	1093	1682 . .	„ 10
1044	1634 . .	June 27	1094	1682 . .	Dec. 31
1045	1635 . .	„ 17	1095	1683 . .	„ 20
1046	1636 . .	„ 5	1096	1684 . .	„ 8
1047	1637 . .	May 26	1097	1685 . .	Nov. 28
1048	1638 . .	„ 15	1098	1686 . .	„ 17
1049	1639 . .	„ 4	1099	1687 . .	„ 7
1050	1640 . .	April 23	1100	1688 . .	Oct. 26

A.H.	A.D.		A.H.	A.D.	
1101	1689 . .	Oct. 15	1151	1738 . .	April 21
1102	1690 . .	„ 5	1152	1739 . .	„ 10
1103	1691 . .	Sept. 24	1153	1740 . .	Mar. 29
1104	1692 . .	„ 12	1154	1741 . .	„ 19
1105	1693 . .	„ 2	1155	1742 . .	„ 8
1106	1694 . .	Aug. 22	1156	1743 . .	Feb. 25
1107	1695 . .	„ 12	1157	1744 . .	„ 15
1108	1696 . .	July 31	1158	1745 . .	„ 3
1109	1697 . .	„ 20	1159	1746 . .	Jan. 24
1110	1698 . .	„ 10	1160	1747 . .	„ 13
1111	1699 . .	June 29	1161	1748 . .	„ 2
1112	1700 . .	„ 18	1162	1748 . .	Dec. 22
1113	1701 . .	„ 8	1163	1749 . .	„ 11
1114	1702 . .	May 28	1164	1750 . .	„ 30
1115	1703 . .	„ 17	1165	1751 . .	Nov. 20
1116	1704 . .	„ 6	1166	1752 . .	„ 8
1117	1705 . .	April 25	1167	1753 . .	Oct. 29
1118	1706 . .	„ 15	1168	1754 . .	„ 18
1119	1707 . .	„ 4	1169	1755 . .	„ 7
1120	1708 . .	Mar. 23	1170	1756 . .	Sept. 26
1121	1709 . .	„ 13	1171	1757 . .	„ 15
1122	1710 . .	„ 2	1172	1758 . .	„ 4
1123	1711 . .	Feb. 19	1173	1759 . .	Aug. 25
1124	1712 . .	„ 9	1174	1760 . .	„ 13
1125	1713 . .	Jan. 28	1175	1761 . .	„ 2
1126	1714 . .	„ 17	1176	1762 . .	July 23
1127	1715 . .	„ 7	1177	1763 . .	„ 12
1128	1715 . .	Dec. 27	1178	1764 . .	„ 1
1129	1716 . .	„ 16	1179	1765 . .	June 20
1130	1717 . .	„ 5	1180	1766 . .	„ 9
1131	1718 . .	Nov. 24	1181	1767 . .	May 30
1132	1719 . .	„ 14	1182	1768 . .	„ 18
1133	1720 . .	„ 2	1183	1769 . .	„ 7
1134	1721 . .	Oct. 22	1184	1770 . .	April 27
1135	1722 . .	„ 12	1185	1771 . .	„ 16
1136	1723 . .	„ 1	1186	1772 . .	„ 4
1137	1724 . .	Sept. 20	1187	1773 . .	Mar. 25
1138	1725 . .	„ 9	1188	1774 . .	„ 14
1139	1726 . .	Aug. 29	1189	1775 . .	„ 4
1140	1727 . .	„ 19	1190	1776 . .	Feb. 21
1141	1728 . .	„ 7	1191	1777 . .	„ 9
1142	1729 . .	July 27	1192	1778 . .	Jan. 30
1143	1730 . .	„ 17	1193	1779 . .	„ 19
1144	1731 . .	„ 6	1194	1780 . .	„ 8
1145	1732 . .	June 24	1195	1780 . .	Dec. 28
1146	1733 . .	„ 14	1196	1781 . .	„ 17
1147	1734 . .	„ 3	1197	1782 . .	„ 7
1148	1735 . .	May 24	1198	1783 . .	Nov. 26
1149	1736 . .	„ 12	1199	1784 . .	„ 14
1150	1737 . .	„ 1	1200	1785 . .	„ 4

A.H.	A.D.	
1201	1786 . .	Oct. 24
1202	1787 . .	„ 13
1203	1788 . .	„ 2
1204	1789 . .	Sept. 21
1205	1790 . .	„ 10
1206	1791 . .	Aug. 31
1207	1792 . .	„ 19
1208	1793 . .	„ 9
1209	1794 . .	July 29
1210	1795 . .	„ 18
1211	1796 . .	„ 7
1212	1797 . .	June 26
1213	1798 . .	„ 15
1214	1799 . .	„ 5
1215	1800 . .	May 25
1216	1801 . .	„ 14
1217	1802 . .	„ 4
1218	1803 . .	April 23
1219	1804 . .	„ 12
1220	1805 . .	„ 1
1221	1806 . .	Mar. 21
1222	1807 . .	„ 11
1223	1808 . .	Feb. 28
1224	1809 . .	„ 16
1225	1810 . .	„ 6
1226	1811 . .	Jan. 26
1227	1812 . .	„ 16
1228	1813 . .	„ 4
1229	1813 . .	Dec. 24
1230	1814 . .	„ 14
1231	1815 . .	„ 3
1232	1816 . .	Nov. 21
1233	1817 . .	„ 11
1234	1818 . .	Oct. 31
1235	1819 . .	„ 20
1236	1820 . .	„ 9
1237	1821 . .	Sept. 28
1238	1822 . .	„ 18
1239	1823 . .	„ 7
1240	1824 . .	Aug. 26
1241	1825 . .	„ 16
1242	1826 . .	„ 5
1243	1827 . .	July 25
1244	1828 . .	„ 14
1245	1829 . .	„ 3
1246	1830 . .	June 22
1247	1831 . .	„ 12
1248	1832 . .	May 31
1249	1833 . .	„ 21
1250	1834 . .	„ 10
1251	1835 . .	April 29
1252	1836 . .	„ 18
1253	1837 . .	„ 7
1254	1838 . .	Mar. 27
1255	1839 . .	„ 17
1256	1840 . .	„ 5
1257	1841 . .	Feb. 23
1258	1842 . .	„ 12
1259	1843 . .	„ 1
1260	1844 . .	Jan. 22
1261	1845 . .	„ 10
1262	1845 . .	Dec. 30
1263	1846 . .	„ 20
1264	1847 . .	„ 9
1265	1848 . .	Nov. 27
1266	1849 . .	„ 17
1267	1850 . .	„ 6
1268	1851 . .	Oct. 27
1269	1852 . .	„ 15
1270	1853 . .	„ 4
1271	1854 . .	Sept. 24
1272	1855 . .	„ 13
1273	1856 . .	„ 1
1274	1857 . .	Aug. 22
1275	1858 . .	„ 11
1276	1859 . .	July 31
1277	1860 . .	„ 20
1278	1861 . .	„ 9
1279	1862 . .	June 29
1280	1863 . .	„ 18
1281	1864 . .	„ 6
1282	1865 . .	May 27
1283	1866 . .	„ 16
1284	1867 . .	„ 5
1285	1868 . .	April 24
1286	1869 . .	„ 13
1287	1870 . .	„ 3
1288	1871 . .	Mar. 23
1289	1872 . .	„ 11
1290	1873 . .	„ 1
1291	1874 . .	Feb. 18
1292	1875 . .	„ 7
1293	1876 . .	Jan. 28
1294	1877 . .	„ 16
1295	1878 . .	„ 5
1296	1878 . .	Dec. 26
1297	1879 . .	„ 15
1298	1880 . .	„ 4
1299	1881 . .	Nov. 23
1300	1882 . .	„ 12

A.H.	A.D.		A.H.	A.D.	
1301	1883 . .	Nov. 2	1310	1892 . .	July 26
1302	1884 . .	Oct. 21	1311	1893 . .	,, 15
1303	1885 . .	,, 10	1312	1894 . .	,, 5
1304	1886 . .	Sept. 30	1313	1895 . .	June 24
1305	1887 . .	,, 19	1314	1896 . .	,, 12
1306	1888 . .	,, 7	1315	1897 . .	,, 2
1307	1889 . .	Aug. 28	1316	1898 . .	May 22
1308	1890 . .	,, 17	1317	1899 . .	,, 12
1309	1891 . .	,, 7	1318	1900 . .	,, 1

NOTE.

The preceding table has been compiled from Professor F. Wüstenfeld's *Vergleichungs-Tabellen der Muhammedanischen und Christlichen Zeitrechnung*, Leipzig, 1854, which are identical with those given in Prinsep's *Useful Tables*, except that Prinsep adopts the English date of changing from the Old (Julian) to the New (Gregorian) style, and consequently omits 11 days on September $\frac{3}{14}$, 1752; while Dr. Wüstenfeld makes the alteration of 9 days on the day when all Catholic Europe adopted the decision of the Bull of Pope Gregory XIII., viz. $\frac{5}{14}$ October, 1582. As this is obviously the most general and proper date for the change of style, I have adopted Dr. Wüstenfeld's principle, and have not deferred a chronological change, which was adopted in 1582 by the chief nations of Europe of the time, until the necessity of the reform had at last been understood in England.

The second column gives the Christian day and month in which the Hijrah year begins.

The Muhammadan year consists of 354 days, with an intercalary day added to the last month eleven times in thirty years (on the 2nd, 5th, 7th, 10th, 13th, 15th, 18th, 21st, 24th, 28th, and 29th years of every thirty years). To find whether the intercalary day is to be added to any given year, divide the year by 30, and if any of the above numbers—2, 5, 7, 10, &c. —remain over, the year is one of 355 days. E.g. 30 divides 1303 forty-three times, with 13 over; therefore the Muhammadan year 1303, corresponding to our 1885-6, will contain 355 days.

To find the exact Christian day corresponding to any given Muhammadan day is a simple matter of calculation. After due regard to the year being Leap-year or not, the Muhammadan equivalent is obtained by reckoning up the days of the month, allowing 30 for Muharram the first month, 29 for Safar the second, and so alternately 30 and 29 to the end, when the intercalary day must be remembered. E.g. 21 November, 1884, is 31 days over the beginning of the Muhammadan year 1302, and would therefore be the 1st of Safar, 1302.

GILBERT AND RIVINGTON, LIMITED, 52, ST JOHN'S SQUARE, LONDON, E.C.

PL. I

MUHAMMAD IBN SÁM, YILDIZ.

PL. II.

ÁRÁM, ALTAMSH, FÍRÓZ I., RIZÍYAH, BAHRÁM.

PL. III.

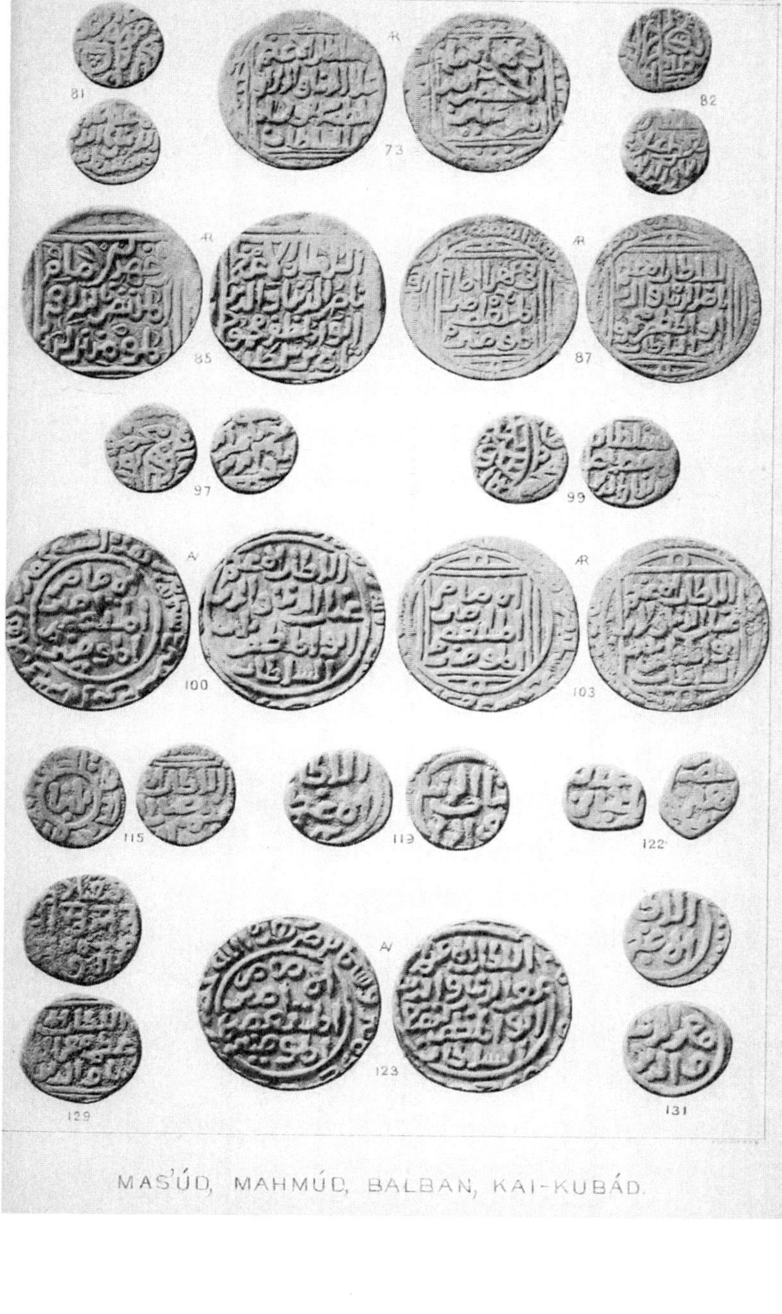

MAS'ÚD, MAHMÚD, BALBAN, KAI-KUBÁD.

PL. IV.

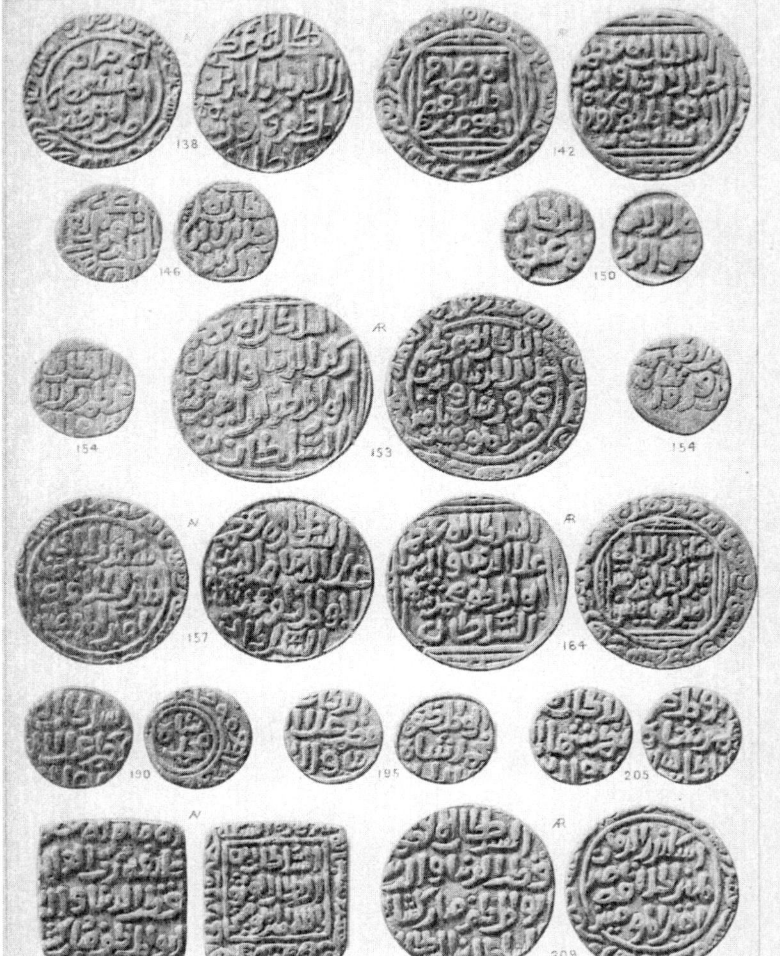

FÍRÓZ II, IBRAHÍM I, MUHAMMAD I, ʾUMAR,
MUBÁRAK I, KHUSRÚ.

PL. V.

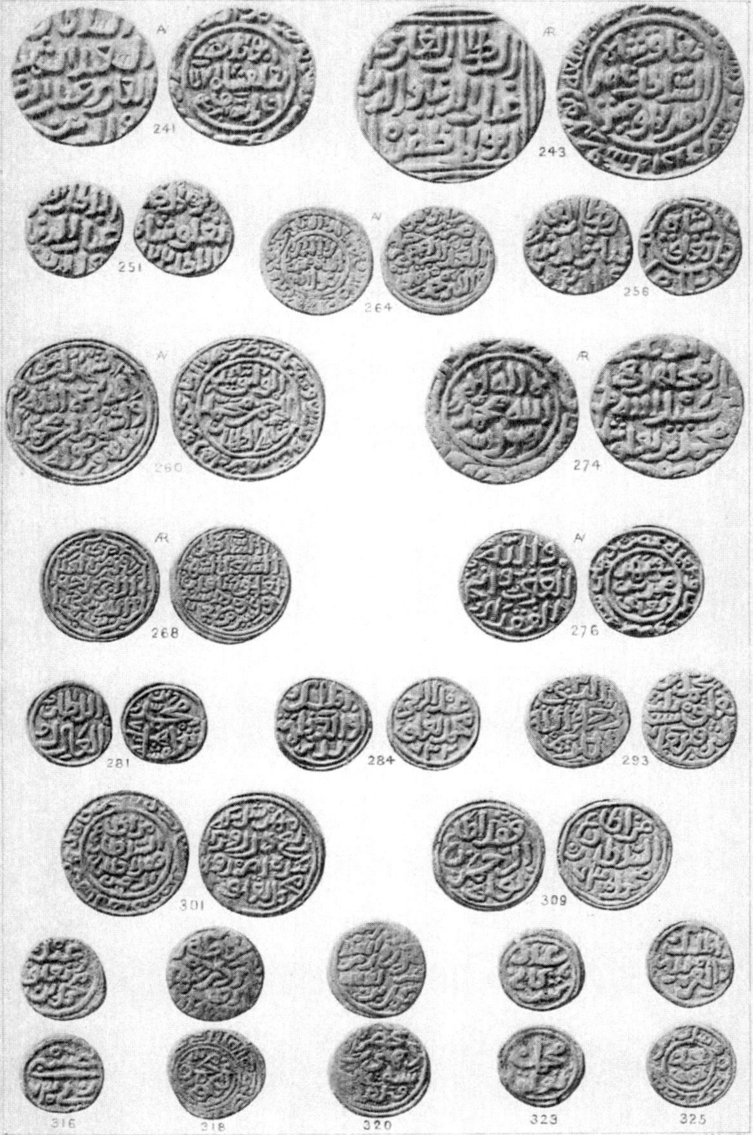

TAGHLAK I. MUHAMMAD IBN TAGHLAK.

PL. VI.

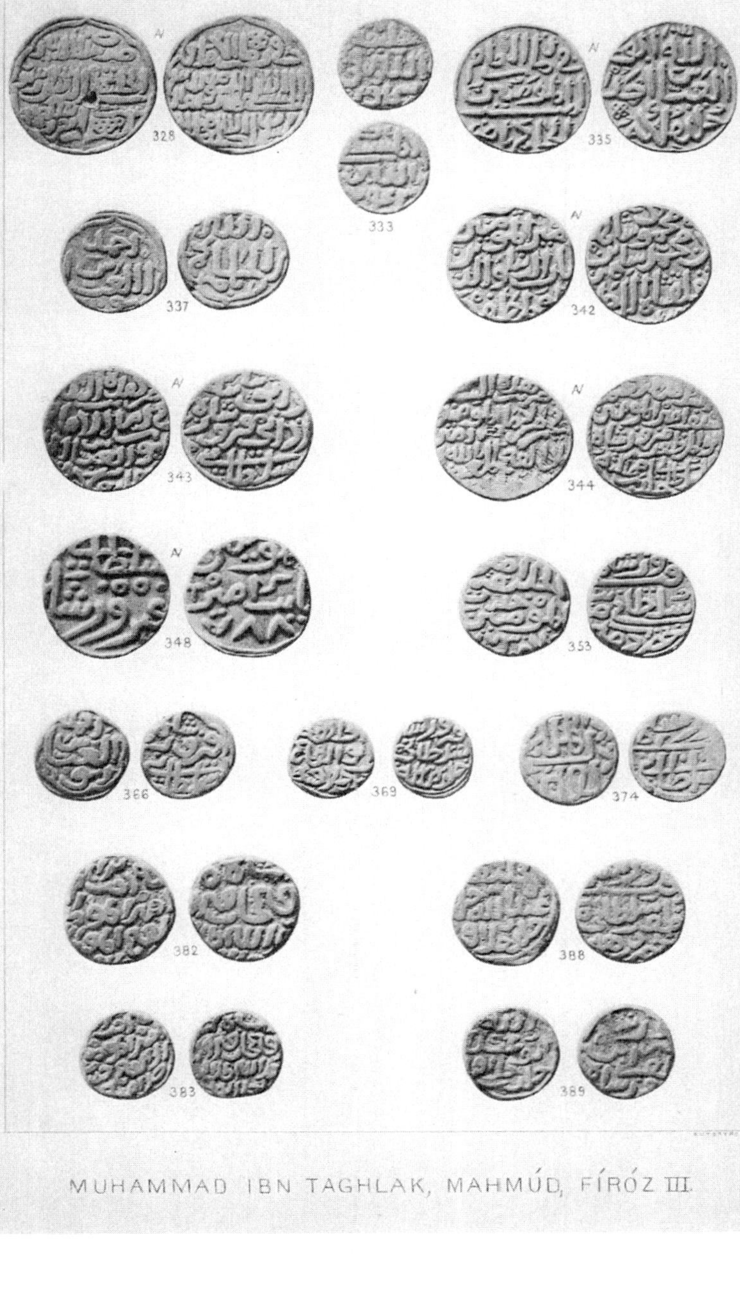

MUHAMMAD IBN TAGHLAK, MAHMÚD, FÍRÓZ III.

PL. VII.

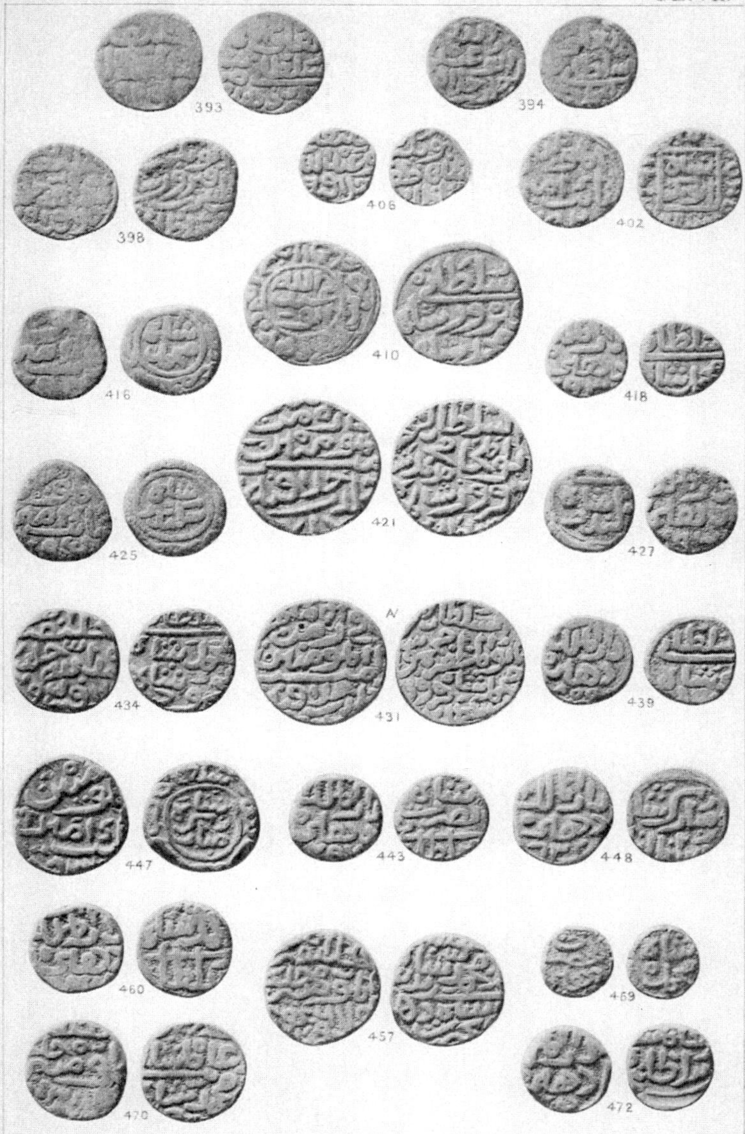

TAGHLAK II, ABU-BAKR, MUHAMMAD III SIKANDAR I,
MAHMÚD II, NASRAT, MUBÁRAK II, MUHAMMAD IV, 'ÁLIM.

PL. VIII.

BUHLÓL, SIKANDAR, IBRÁHÍM LÓDÍ, SHÉR SHÁH.

ISLÁM SHÁH, MUHAMMAD ʿÁDIL, SIKANDAR III.